"Medical doctors are renow[n]... this critique to their general ability... Dresselhaus truly shatters the mold. His book, *Seven Deadly [Lies of] Culture and the Church,* is not only profound but also a joy to read. This is the kind of book you give to your son or daughter before sending them off to university to begin their studies. It is a book pastors and church leaders will use in Sunday School classes and home groups. In short, this is a significant book in the mold of Francis Schaeffer's *A Christian Manifesto,* and it is destined to become an important resource for the global church."

ROBERT P. MENZIES, PHD
New Testament scholar and Missionary
Author of *Christ-Centered* and *The End of History*

"For those who confront daily the 'struggle between truth and lies' of the worldly woke progressive agenda, Dr. Timothy Dresselhaus offers with distinct clarity a much-needed resource of biblical perspective for their effort. He is one of the few who can speak from authority as an experienced medical, academic, and religious professional, researcher, and spiritual leader in helping us understand the competing worldviews that threaten and weaken our faith, our churches, and our faith institutions. He clearly exposes the deceptions and provides a deeper biblical understanding of each of these *Seven Deadly Lies.* I commend this book as a must-read resource and tool for pastors, teachers, and faith leaders in professional settings who are standing firm in godly truth and preaching and teaching a biblical perspective in response to the lies of a woke generation."

JIM JOHNSON, EDD
Professor Emeritus
Department of Psychology and School of Education
Point Loma Nazarene University

"Never in my lifetime has the Church of Jesus faced such an onslaught of lies, the nature of which threaten the integrity of its witness, its ability to transform a culture in chaos, and its very survival. The level of deception has never been this permeative, across mainstream, evangelical, and even Pentecostal expressions of the Church and its institutions. Much like Luke the physician's treatises for the Church, one calling it to the Gospel of Christ and the other to His Spirit at work in His Body, Dr. Timothy Dresselhaus gives us a thoughtful and provocative treatise on seven of the lies Satan is using to destroy the culture around us and Jesus' Church in the Western world. He exposes and refutes the lies with the meticulously documented analysis you would expect of a scholar and scientist, but also calls the Church back to the Word of God in the power of the Spirit as our only rule of faith and life and hope going forward. To quote Dr. Dresselhaus, 'There is no greater darkness than of a church that has lost its way.' And 'No armistice can be negotiated.' This is a spiritual war we must win for the sake of the generations that will follow."

ALEC ROWLANDS, DMIN
Senior Pastor, Westgate Chapel, Seattle, Washington
Founder & President, Church Awakening
Author of *The Presence: Experiencing More of God*

"In *Seven Deadly Lies in the Culture and the Church,* Dr. Timothy Dresselhaus identifies the false belief systems and core values of the dominant Western culture and demonstrates their tragic embrace by many within the church. Though claiming to be nonreligious, the culture's zeal for these lies suggests that they are doctrinal tenets of a false religion and that one cannot embrace a single lie without embracing them all. The author's research reflects the technical nature of his professional and academic background. In addition, his understanding of theology and application of Scripture is sound. *Seven*

Deadly Lies should be on the reading list of every Christian leader and college-age student."

KERMIT S. BRIDGES, DMIN
President
Southwestern Assemblies of God University

Seven Deadly Lies
in the Culture and the Church

Timothy Dresselhaus, MD, MPH

Copyright © 2023 by Timothy R. Dresselhaus, MD, MPH
ALL RIGHTS RESERVED

Published by ACPT Press in cooperation with Kerigma Publications

Cover design by Lauren Short

No portion of this book may be reproduced, stored in a retrieval system, or transmitted in any form or by any means—electronic, mechanical, photocopy, recording, or any other—except for brief quotations in printed reviews, without the prior written permission of the publisher. Write: Permissions, ACPT Press, P.O. Box 11032, Springfield, MO 65808, USA or email: 7DeadlyLies@gmail.com.

Scripture quotations are from The ESV® Bible (The Holy Bible, English Standard Version®), copyright © 2001 by Crossway, a publishing ministry of Good News Publishers. Used by permission. All rights reserved.

Paperback ISBN: 979-8-9873845-0-3
eBook ISBN: 979-8-9873845-1-0

Library of Congress Control Number: 2023902602

*To our son and daughter,
who Shari and I pray will always be true to Christ
by hearing, believing, and obeying his words,
revealed to them in the Bible, the only book that matters.*

Contents

Introduction 11
Chapter 1: Materialism 21
    The Lie in the Culture 21
    The Lie in the Church 25
    The Biblical Truth 29
Chapter 2: Evolutionism 37
    The Lie in the Culture 37
    The Lie in the Church 40
    The Biblical Truth 49
Chapter 3: Relativism 63
    The Lie in the Culture 63
    The Lie in the Church 69
    The Biblical Truth 73
Chapter 4: Abortionism 81
    The Lie in the Culture 81
    The Lie in the Church 86
    The Biblical Truth 91
Chapter 5: Omnisexualism 99
    The Lie in the Culture 99
    The Lie in the Church 104
    The Biblical Truth 112
Chapter 6: Transgenderism 121
    The Lie in the Culture 121
    The Lie in the Church 132
    The Biblical Truth 139
Chapter 7: Communism 147
    The Lie in the Culture 147

    The Lie in the Church..156
    The Biblical Truth 165
Afterward: Biblicism..**171**
Discussion Questions **177**
    Introduction 177
    Chapter 1 – Materialism..177
    Chapter 2 – Evolutionism..178
    Chapter 3 – Relativism..178
    Chapter 4 – Abortionism 179
    Chapter 5 – Omnisexualism 179
    Chapter 6 – Transgenderism 180
    Chapter 7 – Communism 180
    Afterward – Biblicism..181
Acknowledgments..**183**
About the Author...**185**

INTRODUCTION

Did God really say?
Satan, Genesis 3:1

When he lies, he speaks out of his own character, for he is a liar and the father of lies.
Jesus, John 8:44

From the beginning, a spiritual battle has waged between the true and the false, between the Word of God and the lies of Satan. It started in the Garden of Eden, where Satan contradicted God's instructions to Adam and Eve with deceiving words that appealed to their latent pride. This original lie has been retold through the ages, echoing across the millennia to the present. Today, in every domain of the culture, from media and entertainment to education and business, the question is repeated: "Did God really say?"

Lying is what Satan does best. It comes naturally to him since it arises from his lying character and his opposition to God's truth. Satan's track record of accomplishment proves his proficiency. His success, however, comes at a terrible cost to those who believe him. It was death for Adam and Eve; it is death for us. The stakes in this battle are high.

The premise of this book is that an intensifying struggle between truth and lies—a spiritual contest originating in the Garden of Eden and arising from competing worldviews—poses a grave and imminent threat to the church and to the next generation. Christian faith is being challenged by *progressive* lies told not only in the culture but in the church as well. Progressivism rejects a conservative and authoritative view of truth in favor of an evolving one, in which new and novel understandings are sought and advanced. Progressive lies contradict biblical truths while upholding unbiblical falsehoods. As in the Garden, Satan's strategic end is to kill and destroy; progressive lies are his deadly means.

My preparation for this theme began some years ago. I was fortunate to grow up in a spiritually nurturing home and a healthy church, both of which laid the biblical foundations for my subsequent journey. My educational and professional life were entirely in the secular setting, testing but not shaking these foundations. As an undergraduate, I studied modern European intellectual history, broadening my understanding of the prophets of modernity whose nineteenth century philosophical ideas would play out in the popular culture of the twentieth and now twenty-first centuries. Among these were Nietzsche, Schopenhauer, Darwin, Freud, and Marx. While appreciating the significance of these writers, I also recognized the stark contrast between their materialistic, atheistic worldview and my biblical worldview.

Medical school followed at the University of California, San Francisco. I was witness to the earliest days of the human immunodeficiency virus (HIV), a time when the infection was an untreatable death sentence. San Francisco was an epicenter of the initial outbreak given its high concentration of gay men. The sexual culture of San Francisco mirrored its political and religious attitudes, which were progressive and atheistic. Nicaraguan communist Daniel Ortega was a hero, and the majority enthusiastically championed abortion rights. Scripture fortified me to hold fast to a decidedly minority position. An inner-city church that preached the gospel also encouraged me and provided a vibrant Christian community. After completing my residency in Internal Medicine at the University of California, San Diego, I joined the faculty of its School of Medicine, where I have continued to the present.

INTRODUCTION

Early on, I recognized that there were several foundational deceptions that unified the secular academy: 1) man is evolved—along with all forms of life—from a single common ancestor; 2) men and women are free to pursue diverse sexual relationships outside of heterosexual marriage; 3) life may be destroyed prior to birth. This trifecta nullifies foundational truths laid forth in the opening verses of Genesis, namely: 1) God specially created man; 2) God established heterosexual marriage as the singular context for sexual expression; 3) God made man in his image, conferring sacred value on each life from conception. More recently, the academy has added the new lies of transgenderism and revived communism, or neo-Marxism.

Campus culture used to be dismissed as the impractical idealism of gullible students and fringe faculty, as irrelevant to the real world. But that has all changed. The ideas, the rhetoric, and the worldview of the university are now mainstream. The media, corporations, government, and religious institutions wholly embrace them. It is currently the case, as one observer has concluded, that "we all live on campus now."[1]

With this in view, the following chapters delineate seven progressive lies that originate in the academy but now pervade the broader culture in the United States. These lies comprise a web of interconnected deceptions. They build upon and reinforce one another. And they defy God's Word, in particular the opening chapter of Genesis. Each is a variation of Satan's original lie and asks the recurring question, "Did God really say?" They are:

1. *Materialism.* The universe spontaneously happened, and matter came from nothing; there is no God.
2. *Evolutionism.* Man is commonly descended from a single, universal ancestor; God did not create man nor make him in his image.
3. *Relativism.* Truth is subjective and conditional; there are no absolutes.

---

[1] Andrew Sullivan. "We All Live on Campus Now." *New York Intelligencer* (Feb. 9, 2018). https://tinyurl.com/3rh9we5d.

4. *Abortionism.* A mother can murder her child with impunity; God did not create preborn life in his image.
5. *Omnisexualism.* A person may have sex with anyone ("omni" meaning "all"); sexual freedom extends beyond the boundaries of heterosexual marital union.
6. *Transgenderism.* A man is a woman, a woman is a man, and everything is fluid in between; God did not create man as male and female.
7. *Communism.* I am God; there is no other.

That these lies thrive in the broader culture is no surprise. That they thrive in the church is disturbing. A wide swath of the American church, the historic denominations, has already embraced the range of progressive lies. This would include once biblical traditions founded by John Wesley (United Methodist Church), John Calvin (Presbyterian Church (USA)), and Martin Luther (Evangelical Lutheran Church in America). Progressive lies are spreading to the evangelical church where it is increasingly common to find neo-Darwinian evolution promoted as a faithful explanation of origins, gay affirmation as a fair compromise of historic Christian teachings, and communist ideals as an expression of Jesus' core values.

I outline the progressive reality in the contemporary American church in the conceptual framework below. The progressive church holds to a low, critical view of Scripture, adapting teachings to emerging cultural norms and embracing doctrines contrary to historic biblical doctrine (heterodoxy). It looks to science to determine ultimate truth (scientism), incorporating materialism and evolutionism into its worldview. This results in a relativistic perspective on knowledge, truth, and morality, which revises traditional understandings of personhood, sexuality, gender, and society to promote the lies of abortionism, omnisexualism, transgenderism, and communism (neo-Marxism). The biblical church, as guardian of historical and orthodox Christian faith, holds to a high, reverent view of Scripture as the basis of knowledge, truth, and morality. Its worldview reflects God's supernatural activity in the universe's creation, his creation of man in his image with unconditional value, and his design of monogamous, heterosexual marriage to fulfill the first command to "be fruitful and multiply."[2] The biblical church respects the contributions of normal science that have launched rockets to the moon, created life-saving medical treatments, and improved daily life through technological innovation.

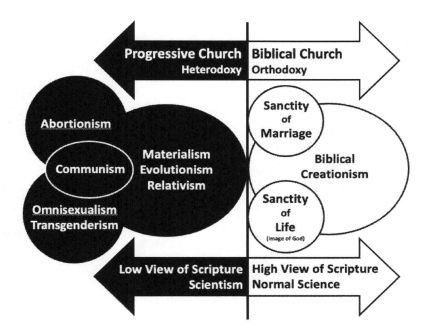

In responding to progressive lies, I would emphasize that this is *not* a book driven by a political agenda. The biblical worldview is preeminent, superseding both culture and politics, which are derivative and contingent. When the Bible speaks truth to the culture, its voice must be amplified. Many pastors are silent on these matters out of fear of being "political." Since progressive lies defy God's Word, they warrant more rather than less attention from the pulpit. Silence is complicity when lies are being told, as there is little difference between not preaching what the Bible contradicts and preaching that contradicts

---

[2] Genesis 1:28.

the Bible. Addressing the cultural forces behind neo-Marxism, transgenderism, and abortionism, author Eric Metaxas warns:

> One of the principal ways in which they have gained strength is in persuading so many in the American Church that to fight them is to abandon the "Gospel" for pure culture warring or for politics. This is not just nonsense, but is a supremely deceptive and satanic lie, designed only to silence those who would genuinely speak for truth.[3]

This is *not* a book about minor issues that are peripheral to the gospel. God's Word encompasses the totality of Scripture from Genesis to Revelation; the story of redemption is told from cover to cover. It is, in its entirety, a revelation of God's truth. Genesis—the inspired work of Moses—is the foundation of the gospel. If progressive lies erode this foundation, the gospel collapses and ceases to make any sense. Jesus affirmed this when he corrected his detractors: "For if you believed Moses, you would believe me; for he wrote of me. But if you do not believe his writings, how will you believe my words?"[4]

This book does *not* judge the spiritual standing of those who, wittingly or unwittingly, tell progressive lies. That is God's responsibility, not mine. But what is certain is that these lies have caused and will continue to cause spiritual destruction. It is discernment, not judgmentalism, to identify and oppose deceptions that undermine the authority of Scripture and challenge sound biblical doctrine.

This book *is* an urgent call to believe biblically, think biblically, and act biblically. God calls us to hear his Word, to believe his Word, and to obey his Word. God explains this priority to Joshua in this way: "This Book of the Law shall not depart from your mouth, but you shall meditate on it day and night, so that you may be careful to do according to all that is written in it. For then you will make your way prosperous, and then you will have good success."[5] The writer of Hebrews reminds

---

[3] Eric Metaxas. *Letter to the American Church* (Washington, DC: Salem Books, 2022), xii.
[4] John 5:46-47.

INTRODUCTION

us that no place is beyond its probing reach: "For the word of God is living and active, sharper than any two-edged sword, piercing to the division of soul and of spirit, of joints and of marrow, and discerning the thoughts and intentions of the heart."[6] To those who argue that God's ancient words have expired and do not pertain to contemporary issues, Jesus adds, "Heaven and earth will pass away, but my words will not pass away."[7]

How can the next generation remain true to Christ and persevere in the face of challenges to their faith? By knowing and obeying Jesus' words. Many have succumbed to progressive lies precisely because the church has failed to contend for biblical truth or to connect young minds and hearts to a durable Christian faith rooted in Scripture. Not that some will not leave the faith even under the best of circumstances. But such outcomes are not a reason to shrink from the battle. To paraphrase author Andrew Klavan, "Of course, we may lose the fight. But you can't win a surrender."[8]

By every measure, Alisa Childers was a devout Christian. Building upon a childhood decision to accept Christ as her Savior, she immersed herself in the life of the church, witnessed to her unsaved friends, participated in missions' trips, and even toured as a member of a Christian band. A crisis arose when her faith, "intellectually weak and untested," was challenged not by an atheist, a college professor, or a false religionist but by a progressive pastor.

> This was an educated, intellectual, calm, and eloquent church leader—someone who expressed love for Jesus. He was a brilliant communicator, and he had a bone to pick with Christianity. Meeting after meeting, every precious belief I held about God, Jesus, and the Bible was placed on the intellectual chopping block and hacked to pieces.[9]

---

[5] Joshua 1:8.
[6] Hebrews 4:12.
[7] Matthew 24:35.
[8] Andrew Klavan. https://tinyurl.com/yss4z6af.
[9] Alisa Childers. *Another Gospel? A Lifelong Christian Seeks Truth in Response to Progressive Christianity* (Carol Stream, Illinois: Tyndale House, 2020), 6.

Unlike many, Alisa's crisis had a hopeful ending as she rebuilt her faith upon the reliable Word of God. But her story is a cautionary warning that progressive lies are pervasive and destructive.

Against the secularizing influences in the church, Harry Blamires—Anglican theologian and mentee of C.S. Lewis—calls for a "Christian mind" that regards truth as objective, authoritative, and God-given. The Christian mind belongs to anyone who hears, believes, and obeys God's Word, not just to intellectuals or the well-educated. Discerning the difference between truth and lies does not require an advanced degree in physics, biology, history, ethics, or theology. It only requires a simple, believing embrace of Scripture in its most straight-forward sense. Blamires elaborates on the distinctive truth that animates the Christian mind:

> The marks of truth as Christianly conceived, then, are that it is supernaturally grounded, not developed within nature; that it is objective and not subjective; that it is a revelation and not a construction; that it is discovered by inquiry and not elected by a majority vote; that it is authoritative and not a matter of personal choice.[10]

My prayer is that the chapters ahead will help leaders, pastors, parents, educators, and students to think biblically and to speak biblically wherever truth is contested, whether in the culture or in the church. The eternal destiny of the next generation is in the balance. That is why I have often repeated this protective principle to my son and daughter as they have grown into adulthood:

> No matter what the President or the Supreme Court say; no matter what the science or the culture say; no matter what your teachers or your classmates say; no matter what X or ChatGPT say; no matter what your pastor or your youth leader say; no

---

[10] Harry Blamires. *The Christian Mind: How Should a Christian Think?* (Vancouver: Regent College, 2005), Loc 1404, Kindle.

INTRODUCTION

matter what your grandparents or your sibling say; and *no matter what I say* ... if it in any way contradicts God's Word, if it contradicts the Bible, don't believe it!

CHAPTER 1
MATERIALISM

Spontaneous creation is the reason there is something rather than nothing, why the universe exists, why we exist. It is not necessary to invoke God.[11]

Stephen Hawking

In the beginning, God created the heavens and the earth.

Genesis 1:1

THE LIE IN THE CULTURE

Through time, people have speculated on the most basic and important question: how did the heavens and the earth, the cosmos, come to exist? Why is there something rather than nothing? The answer to this question is vital to how we view God, ourselves, one another, and the world in which we live. It is vital to meaning, purpose, morality, knowledge, and truth. The question is so important that God answers it in the first verse of the first book of the Bible, and it is so important that Satan has tirelessly promoted a false counter-narrative to distract people from the truth.

Scientific materialism is the prevailing lie in western culture. To the cosmological question of the origin of the universe, Carl Sagan gives this famous answer: "The cosmos is all that is or was or ever will be."[12]

---

[11] Stephen Hawking. *The Grand Design* (New York: Random House, 2010), 179.
[12] Carl Sagan. "Cosmos: A Personal Journey." Public Broadcasting System, 1980.

Scientific materialism claims that matter, governed by physical laws, is the essential reality, from the smallest subatomic particles to the far-flung galaxies. It is the all-sufficient explanation for everything. Physics dictates our collective meaning and purpose; physics decides ultimate knowledge and truth.

Scientific materialism denies the existence of God. It is atheistic. A generation of "new atheists," prominent among them physicist Stephen Hawking and biologist Richard Dawkins, have peddled naturalistic explanations of origins under the guise of science and with full confidence in God's non-existence. In cosmology, Hawking argues that matter explains the origin of the universe; in biology, Dawkins argues that matter explains the evolution of man. God is irrelevant in either case.

The conflict between atheistic science and biblical Christianity did not always exist. The Judeo-Christian worldview gave birth to the western scientific tradition, believing the universe to be an orderly reflection of the mind of God and therefore amenable to rational, scientific inquiry. Most significant scientists prior to the nineteenth century—among them Galileo, Copernicus, and Newton—were theists, not atheists. For them, science was a reason *for* faith, not *against* faith.

This has all changed. Scientific materialism's ascent has corresponded to a decline in religious faith across the west. The broader culture now widely believes the lie conceived by faculty at leading research universities. In Europe, empty churches attest to the collapse of religion. A similar collapse is under way in the United States. A Gallup poll of religious attitudes has tracked a steady decline in the proportion of respondents who consider religion "very important," falling below 50 percent for the first time in 2020. Seventy-eight percent believe "religion as a whole is losing its influence on American life"; more than a quarter regard the Bible as "fables" or "legends."[13] The Pew Research Center has measured a similar secularizing shift, focusing on a growing number of "nones," individuals with no religious affiliation. The researchers observe that "about three-in-ten U.S. adults (29 percent) are religious 'nones,' people who are atheists, agnostics, or 'nothing in

---

[13] "Religion." *Gallup News*. https://tinyurl.com/mxs7z4wr.

particular' when asked about religious identity."[14] A Gallup poll completed in 2022 confirmed these worrisome findings, with a growing proportion of U.S. adults (19 percent) denying any belief in God; atheistic identification was highest among those 18 to 29 years old (32 percent) and ideologically liberal (38 percent).[15]

What are the materialistic claims that persuade so many? For this we turn first to Stephen Hawking, who is among the new atheists' most articulate spokespersons. Hawking's career is remarkable and courageous, suffering as he did from a slowly progressive form of amyotrophic lateral sclerosis (ALS), to which he succumbed in 2018. A theoretical physicist and cosmologist, he was, at the time of his death, the director of research at the Centre for Theoretical Cosmology at the University of Cambridge. In 2010, he published with Leonard Mlodinow the New York Times best-selling book, *The Grand Design*, in which he offers his explanation of the beginning of the universe.

Hawking argues that philosophy and religion have failed to keep pace with scientific progress, particularly in physics. Thus, scientists are the "bearers of the torch of discovery in our quest for knowledge."[16] Most illuminating are the recent discoveries in quantum physics, which have transformed prior conceptions of the universe and led to the notion that "the universe itself has no single history, nor even an independent existence."[17] He then posits the ultimate theory of everything, the M-theory, which holds that ours is one of many universes and is neither original nor unique. The number of universes in the "multiverse," according to Hawking, is incomprehensible, on the order of 10^{500} (1 followed by 500 zeroes). The punchline quickly follows:

> M-theory predicts that a great many universes were created out of nothing. Their creation does not require the intervention of some supernatural being or god. Rather, these multiple universes arise

---

[14] Gregory A. Smith. "About Three-in-Ten U.S. Adults Are Now Religiously Unaffiliated." Pew Research Center (Dec. 14, 2021). https://tinyurl.com/58kjptxn.

[15] Jeffrey M. Jones. "Belief in God in U.S. Dips to 81%, a New Low." *Gallup News* (Jun. 17, 2022). https://tinyurl.com/2uuvyb95.

[16] Hawking, *The Grand Design*, 9.

[17] Hawking, *The Grand Design*, 15.

naturally from physical law. They are a prediction of science. [Thus] our presence selects out from this vast array only those universes that are compatible with our existence. Although we are puny and insignificant on the scale of the cosmos, this makes us in a sense the lords of creation.

The implications of Hawking's speculations are profound. Having dispensed with God, he disallows anything supernatural, anything outside of the operation of physical laws. He also asserts that human behavior is determined, so "it seems we are no more than biological machines and that free will is just an illusion."[18] The endless possibilities within a multiverse turn reality on its head. Hawking compares this to the science fiction film, *The Matrix*, in which people are pawns in a simulated environment, ignorant of the boundaries or artifice of their reality. By analogy, any individual's reality is merely one among an infinite number of possibilities. "We are all," Hawking states, "figments of someone else's dream."[19] The multiverse has even made it to the big screen, captured in the title of *Doctor Strange in the Multiverse of Madness* (2022) and thematically incorporated into the Spider-Man and Avengers series.

Hawking is not alone in his materialistic cosmology or in his conclusions. Lawrence Krauss, a Canadian-American astrophysicist, insists from quantum theory that our universe could have arisen from nothing, as suggested by the title and subtitle of his best-selling book, *A Universe from Nothing: Why There Is Something Rather than Nothing*. He proposes that space emptied of everything—matter and radiation—still weighs something and makes up a special nothing. This empty space is not actually empty, filled as it is with dark energy, or dark matter, which contributes significantly to the overall mass of the universe. Krauss concludes it is from this energy-filled void that the universe may have evolved. However, he seems to contradict his book's title when he concedes, "It certainly seems sensible to imagine that, a priori, matter cannot arise from empty space, so that *something*, in this

---

[18] Hawking, *The Grand Design*, 35.
[19] Hawking, *The Grand Design*, 44.

sense, cannot arise from *nothing*."[20] In his foreword to *A Universe from Nothing*, astrophysicist Neil deGrasse Tyson also undermines Krauss' stated premise: "Nothing is not nothing. Nothing is something. That's how a cosmos can be spawned from the void."[21]

While readers may find Krauss' cosmology semantically confusing, his hostility toward a theistic worldview is unambiguous. "When it comes to understanding how our universe evolves," he argues, "religion and theology have been at best irrelevant. They often muddy the waters, for example, by focusing on questions of nothingness without providing any definition of the term based on empirical evidence."[22]

THE LIE IN THE CHURCH

While the progressive church may distance itself from the atheistic aspect of the cosmologies of Hawking or Krauss, it has contributed to their spread by destroying biblical cosmology and creating a vacuum which such views move quickly to fill. It has replaced faith-filled biblicism with uncritical scientism, placing unwarranted trust in the power of scientific methods and knowledge. It has elevated the human intellect above the authority of Scripture, substituting a supernatural conception of the universe's origin with a naturalistic one. It has continued the efforts begun in the nineteenth century to undermine confidence in the Bible as a reliable source of truth and knowledge.

Peter Enns is an American theologian who has written extensively from an evangelical perspective about the interface of the Bible and science. In 2005, he published his most important work, *Inspiration and Incarnation: Evangelicals and the Problem of the Old Testament*. While acclaimed by many within the evangelical community, it also triggered controversy, especially regarding its view of biblical inerrancy. The ensuing divisions within the Reformed community led to his separation from Westminster Theological Seminary, an institution founded by J.

---

[20] Lawrence M. Krauss. *A Universe from Nothing: Why There Is Something Rather than Nothing* (New York: Atria, 2010), 151.

[21] Neil deGrasse Tyson in Krauss, *A Universe from Nothing*, Foreward.

[22] Krauss, *A Universe from Nothing*, Preface.

Gresham Machen almost a century before precisely in reaction to views such as Enns'.

Enns describes himself as a "progressive inerrantist," one who is sensitive to the ancient genres and conventions of biblical literature but skeptical of literalistic readings. In this view, "things like historical inaccuracies, myth, and theological diversity in Scripture are not errors needing to be explained away or minimized but, paradoxically, embraced as divine wisdom."[23] Enns eagerly embraces a century and a half of critical scholarship to support his perspective, concluding that "when new evidence comes to light, or old evidence is seen in a new light, we must be willing to engage that evidence and adjust our doctrine accordingly."[24] He further subtracts from the authority of Scripture by making this analogy to the Incarnation: "As Christ is both God and human, so is the Bible. In other words, we are to think of the Bible analogously to how Christians think about Jesus … In the same way that Jesus is—*must be*—both God and human, the Bible is also a divine and human book."[25]

Where does Enns settle on Genesis? With other critical scholars, he times the authorship of Genesis to the sixth century before Christ and draws parallels to *Enuma Elish*, the "Babylonian Genesis," relegating Genesis to the status of myth along with other creation narratives which share "an ancient, premodern, prescientific way of addressing questions of ultimate origins and meaning in the form of stories."[26] "It is a fundamental misunderstanding of Genesis," he concludes, "to expect it to answer questions generated by a modern worldview."[27] Enns is torchbearer in our day of the progressive side of the fundamentalist-modernist controversy that tore apart the Presbyterian Church in the early twentieth century before spreading to other mainline denominations. This side, from Machen's perspective, is "rooted in naturalism—that is, in the denial of any entrance of the creative power

---

[23] Peter Enns. *Inspiration and Incarnation: Evangelicals and the Problem of the Old Testament* (Grand Rapids, Michigan: Baker, 2015), Preface to 2nd edition.

[24] Enns, *Inspiration and Incarnation*, 2.

[25] Enns, *Inspiration and Incarnation*, 5.

[26] Enns, *Inspiration and Incarnation*, 29.

[27] Enns, *Inspiration and Incarnation*, 44.

of God (as distinguished from the ordinary course of nature) in connection with the origin of Christianity."[28]

With Hawking and Krauss, Enns believes the Bible is irrelevant to cosmology, to understanding the beginning of the universe as described in Genesis. His sense of biblical irrelevance has expanded considerably over time. His pessimism over the trustworthiness of God's Word reaches despair a short eleven years after *Inspiration and Incarnation's* original publication.

> My faith had transformed from "I know what I believe" to "I think I know." Then, as if bicycling down a steep hill with no brakes, it moved more quickly to
>
> *I think I thought I knew,*
> *I'm not so sure anymore,*
> *I don't really know anymore,*
> *Honestly, I have no idea,*
> *Leave me alone.*[29]

In the long-standing tension between special (biblical) revelation and general (natural) revelation, Enns places the general above the special, the inferences of science above the teachings of Scripture. Enns is not alone bicycling down the slippery slope nor is his perspective unique to the academy. Other progressive Christians have reached the same conclusion. Former Vineyard USA pastor Ken Wilson has embraced scientism enthusiastically. Leading an Ann Arbor congregation in the shadow of the University of Michigan, he promotes Blue Ocean Church on their website as "Jesus-centered, progressive" and "science friendly."[30] His lesbian co-pastor is a student of "creation stories." The pastoral team's interests extend beyond critical biblical scholarship to "evolutionary science," "environmental science," "social sciences," and

---

[28] J. Gresham Machen. *Christianity and Liberalism*. (Warrendale, Pennsylvania: Ichthus Publications, 2020), Loc 101, Kindle.

[29] Peter Enns. *The Sin of Certainty: Why God Desires Our Trust More Than Our "Correct" Beliefs* (New York: Harper Collins, 2016), 14.

[30] Blue Ocean Church. https://www.a2blue.org/.

"women and gender studies." Blue Ocean Church is indeed science friendly, in the most fawning and unbiblical sense.

The First United Methodist Church near our home stands along a well-traveled, major freeway. The arches of its beautiful sanctuary rise above the valley floor in which it is situated. Illuminated signage flashes its priorities to the community: "End Hate," "Bless the Animals," and, every June, the multicolored gay-pride flag; messages about God or from the Bible are conspicuously absent. In a recent sermon on science and religion, Pastor Trudy Robinson sheds light on how her church got to this place. She places the Genesis account in the category of allegory along with the Babylonian narrative upon which she believes it is based. She places this against the "objective" claims of science and ends in a subjectivity that is doubtful of Genesis but confident in science.

> I seek the way in which new possibilities are created within me and through me even in the midst of chaos, like in Genesis, or violence, like in Babylon. I couldn't find peace in the world if this was not a part of my truth … My truth comes from science, and because I believe in science, I listen to and seek information from people who are much smarter than I who have spent much more time studying things that I know nothing about.[31]

Robinson's retreat from biblicism is not unusual in the pulpit these days. Along with Blue Ocean Church, First United Methodist Church is the new progressive norm: science friendly, Bible hostile. And their numbers are growing.

What if Hawking and Enns, Krauss and Wilson, Tyson and Robinson are correct? What if Genesis has nothing to say about what happened at the beginning of the universe? If so, it would be pointless for you to read further or for me to write further. We would have to confess, in Hawking's words, that we are the lord of creation, not Jesus. But they are lying.

---

[31] Trudy Robinson. "Science and Religion," Jun. 21, 2020. https://tinyurl.com/3buh8m57.

The Biblical Truth

"In the beginning, God created the heavens and the earth."[32] This is the biblical truth, telling us in ten words how the universe came to be, why there is something rather than nothing. It is clear, direct, and unambiguous. It is easy to understand, accessible to the child and the adult, the unschooled and the educated. Its veracity supports the authority of all that follows. It is a cornerstone that upholds the integrity of Scripture.

In rebuttal to scientific materialism, Genesis declares that God, not matter, is preexistent and eternal. Before anything existed, God was. He is the one who was then, who is now, and who always will be. Nothing is before him or after him; nothing is above him or beyond him. He is supreme and preeminent. He is all powerful, all knowing, all present. He is Creator.

Genesis tells us that the universe had a beginning. Before God spoke the cosmos into existence, there was nothing. There was no matter, no time, no space. The stars of the galaxies and the quarks of the atom were all created *ex nihilo*—out of nothing. The writer of Hebrews explains it succinctly: "By faith we understand that the universe was created by the word of God, so that what is seen was not made out of things that are visible."[33] Thus began the universe. God spoke at the beginning, and all that is—matter, time, space—came into existence. Something did indeed come from nothing, by the power of his Word.

The prologue to the Gospel of John mirrors the opening of Genesis, underscoring that the doctrine of creation unifies all of Scripture. "In the beginning was the Word, and the Word was with God, and the Word was God. He was in the beginning with God. All things were made through him, and without him was not any thing made that was made."[34] John reiterates that the universe had a beginning and that it had a Creator. The Creator is the eternal Word (*logos*), none other than Jesus. We know that all things were made through Jesus; nothing would exist

---

[32] Genesis 1:1.
[33] Hebrews 11:3.
[34] John 1:1-3.

but for him. The heavens and the earth rest upon the person of Christ, who not only speaks truth but also embodies truth. Sound doctrine always begins by acknowledging that Jesus created the universe *ex nihilo* by his powerful Word.

Jesus' role in the universe's creation establishes his deity and Lordship. Paul's letter to the Colossians, intended to encourage sound doctrine at a time when false teachings were common, emphasizes what orthodox Christology looks like.

> He is the image of the invisible God, the firstborn of all creation. For by him all things were created, in heaven and on earth, visible and invisible, whether thrones or dominions or rulers or authorities—all things were created through him and for him. And he is before all things, and in him all things hold together.[35]

For Paul, Jesus' preeminence in creation is the basis for his preeminence in redemption. He is both "the firstborn of all creation" and "the firstborn of the dead."[36] The two go hand in hand. The one without the other is simply not possible. To reject Jesus as Creator is to reject Jesus as Savior.

There is a future day when we will be held to account for what we believe. I wonder if the progressives, whether scientific materialists or progressive inerrantists, will hear the same thundering voice that answered Job's speculations about matters beyond his understanding: "Where were you when I laid the foundation of the earth?"[37] I, for one, do not want to stand beside those who have substituted lies for truth, man's insights for God's revelation. By contrast, those who have accepted Jesus as the one who creates *and* who saves will be prepared to sing the heavenly anthem that will ring throughout eternity:

> Holy, holy, holy, is the Lord God Almighty
> who was and is and is to come!

---

[35] Colossians 1:15-17.
[36] Colossians 1:18.
[37] Job 38:4.

> Worthy are you, our Lord and God,
> to receive glory and honor and power,
> for you created all things,
> and by your will they existed and were created.[38]

The early church emphasized biblical teaching on the origins of the universe. Michael Kruger is an American theologian and Professor of New Testament and Early Christianity at the Reformed Theological Seminary. He has examined the very earliest development of Christian doctrine, which was closely connected to apostolic teaching and to the emergence of the canon of the New Testament. He identifies seven early, second-century Christian beliefs common across multiple "rules of faith" that restate priority doctrines of the Bible.

1. There is one God, the Creator of heaven and earth.
2. This same God spoke through the prophets of the Old Testament regarding the coming Messiah.
3. Jesus is the Son of God, born from the seed of David, through the virgin Mary.
4. Jesus is the Creator of all things, who came into the world, God in the flesh.
5. Jesus came to bring salvation and redemption for those who believe in him.
6. Jesus physically suffered and was crucified under Pontius Pilate, raised bodily from the dead, and exalted to the right hand of God the Father.
7. Jesus will return again to judge the world.[39]

Of these doctrinal statements, two (numbers 1 and 4) underscore an early commitment to the plain understanding of Genesis 1:1 and to the apostolic teaching that Jesus is the Creator of all things, as taught in John's Gospel and Paul's epistles. These statements would chart the

---

[38] Revelation 4:8,11.
[39] Michael J. Kruger. *Christianity at the Crossroads: How the Second Century Shaped the Future of the Church* (Downers Grove, Illinois: Intervarsity, 2018), 65.

course of orthodox doctrine for the centuries to follow, serving as a reference for what biblical Christians have believed through the ages to the present.

Kruger's summary reflects the Epistle of Diognetus, a mid-second-century defense of Christian beliefs and practices. In keeping with the prologue to John's Gospel, the unknown author contends that the Creator of the universe and the heaven-sent Son are one and the same.

> For, as I said, this was no mere earthly invention which was delivered to them, nor is it a mere human system of opinion, which they judge it right to preserve so carefully, nor has a dispensation of mere human mysteries been committed to them, but truly God Himself, who is almighty, the Creator of all things, and invisible, has sent from heaven, and placed among men, [Him who is] the truth, and the holy and incomprehensible Word, and has firmly established Him in their hearts. He did not, as one might have imagined, send to men any servant, or angel, or ruler, or any one of those who bear sway over earthly things, or one of those to whom the government of things in the heavens has been entrusted, but the very Creator and Fashioner of all things—by whom He made the heavens.[40]

The sufficient reason for New Testament and second-century Christians to believe that "in the beginning, God created the heavens and the earth" is that God's true and inerrant Word says so, and what it says is what it means. It is how they knew then and how we know now what is true: "for the Bible tells me so." To comprehend truth, nothing more is required. However, there are lines of evidence that confirm the revelation of Scripture. Scientific progress over the last two centuries is finally catching up with the biblical cosmology first revealed to the Hebrews over three millennia ago.

Until recently, skeptics of the Genesis account argued that the universe and matter were eternal. This is no longer the case. That the

---

[40] Unknown, transl. Alexander Roberts and James Donaldson. "Epistle to Diognetus," 5-6. https://tinyurl.com/4nnsd69p.

universe had a beginning is settled science, which is very unsettling to materialists who had held that matter, not God, was preexistent. An early hint came from the observations of nineteenth-century German astronomer Henrich Olbers, who noted that starlight in the night sky was not uniform but interspersed with dark regions. Known as Olbers' Paradox, this contradicted the expectation were the universe infinite, in which case the night sky would be entirely illuminated, and no dark regions would remain.[41] In the early twentieth century, astrophysicist Fred Hubble observed a "red shift" when looking at the spectrum of light coming from remote stars and galaxies. This shift is analogous to the Doppler effect commonly appreciated when the sound pitch emitted by a moving object—for instance, the siren of an emergency vehicle—changes based on whether it is coming toward or moving away from the observer. The red shift led physicists reluctantly to conclude that the universe is expanding ("galactic recession") and therefore had a beginning.[42]

When Albert Einstein, who had long contended for an infinite, eternal universe, visited Hubble in 1931 to look for himself at the astronomical evidence, he publicly acknowledged that the universe had a "beginning."[43] The implications were profound and, for materialists, alarming. In line with the inescapable logic of the Kalam cosmological argument,

> Everything that begins to exist has a cause.
> The universe began to exist.
> The universe has a cause.

Put differently, a finite universe is expected if it were created by an infinite God. As physicist and Nobel Laureate Arno Penzias comments, "The best data we have are exactly what I would have predicted, had I nothing to go on but the five Books of Moses, the Psalms, the Bible as a whole."[44]

---

[41] Stephen C. Meyer. *Return of the God Hypothesis: Three Scientific Discoveries that Reveal the Mind Behind the Universe* (New York: Harper Collins, 2021), 85.

[42] Meyer, *Return of the God Hypothesis*, 109.

[43] Meyer, *Return of the God Hypothesis*, 122.

Equally problematic for the materialists is mounting evidence that the universe is finely tuned. Physical laws with precise parameters govern the universe. Even a minute adjustment to any of these parameters—the gravitational constant, the weak and strong nuclear forces, the electromagnetic force, the cosmological constant, among others—would cause the universe to unravel. That the universe is balanced on this knife-edge points to an intelligent and powerful Creator. These "cosmic coincidences" forced physicist and atheist Fred Hoyle to admit:

> A common-sense interpretation of the facts suggests that a super-intellect has monkeyed with physics, as well as chemistry and biology, and that there are no blind forces worth speaking about in nature. The numbers one calculates from the facts seem to me so overwhelming as to put this conclusion almost beyond question.[45]

The fine tuning of the universe fulfills the two criteria of intelligent design proposed by William Dembski: extreme improbability and patterned specificity.[46] As Hoyle acknowledges, it is enormously improbable that multiple physical parameters would randomly achieve the required precision to support the known universe. It is not by chance that the universe displays a recognizable pattern, or specificity, across atomic and cosmic structures. This is analogous to the letters on this page, which are improbably arranged but also patterned in a way to communicate information, both indicators of intelligent cause. The evidence of improbability and specificity in the universe's order is not a surprise as language is embedded not only in this book but in God's design of the cosmos. God used language to create the universe: "By the word of the LORD the heavens were made, and by the breath of his mouth all their host."[47] The heavens, in turn, speak to us of God's creative power:

---

[44] Meyer, *Return of the God Hypothesis*, 297.
[45] Meyer, *Return of the God Hypothesis*, 174.
[46] William A. Demski. *The Design Inference: Eliminating Chance Through Small Probabilities* (Cambridge: Cambridge University Press, 1998), 33-36.

MATERIALISM

> The heavens declare the glory of God,
> and the sky above proclaims his handiwork.
> Day to day pours out speech,
>   and night to night reveals knowledge.
> There is no speech, nor are there words,
>   whose voice is not heard.
> Their voice goes out through all the earth,
>   and their words to the end of the world. [48]

That the universe had a beginning and is finely tuned points clearly to God's activity. But to what purpose? Since Copernicus' discovery in 1543 that the earth revolves around the sun and not the sun around the earth, humanity's perceived significance has steadily plummeted to the level of a cosmic accident. The science is increasingly clear, however, that God's ultimate purpose in finely tuning the universe is precisely to accommodate abundant and diverse forms of life, and in particular the human species, restoring man to his central place in the cosmos. This is the basis of the anthropic principle, the idea that the structure and materials of the universe, the physical laws that govern them, and the values of physical constants anticipate human existence. The fit between cosmic structure and biological requirements leads astrophysicist Freeman Dyson to concede, "I do not feel like an alien in this universe. The more I examine the universe and study the details of its architecture, the more evidence I find that the universe in some sense must have known that we were coming."[49]

Cosmic-biologic fit is displayed throughout nature, including, as one example among many, the human circulation. During a typical lifetime, the heart will beat over two billion times, propelling blood forward by the coordinated contraction of cardiac muscle comprised of billions of muscle cells filled with trillions of contractile filaments. Each contraction pumps one hundred billion red blood cells through hundreds

---

[47] Psalm 33:6.
[48] Psalm 19:1-4.
[49] Freeman Dyson. *Disturbing the Universe* (New York: Basic Books, 1979), 250.

of miles of tiny capillaries to deliver vital oxygen, loosely bound to an iron atom in each red cell's hemoglobin, to the target tissue. During their one-hundred-twenty-day life span, red blood cells squeeze through capillaries sometimes half their diameter. This deformity requires red cell softness a hundred times that of latex and a strength exceeding that of steel. This elegant, complex process would not be possible without radiation emitted by the sun through a transparent atmosphere to trigger the photosynthetic production of oxygen, not to mention the availability of elements such as oxygen, hydrogen, and iron or the fluid properties of water.[50] Such improbability and specificity would not be possible without God. "On these grounds and others like them one is driven to think that whatever else may be true," observes C.S. Lewis, "the popular scientific cosmology at any rate is certainly not."[51]

Having telescoped in from the galaxies to mankind, it is appropriate next to address the related and arguably more important question: "How did man get here?"

---

[50] Michael Denton. *The Miracle of Man: The Fine Tuning of Nature for Human Existence* (Seattle, Washington: Discovery Institute Press, 2022), 30-33.

[51] John G. West. "An Argument from C.S. Lewis for Intelligent Design." *Evolution News & Science Today* (Nov. 18, 2022). https://tinyurl.com/mrx23fwa.

CHAPTER 2
EVOLUTIONISM

Far from pointing to a designer, the illusion of design in the living world is explained with far greater economy and with devastating elegance by Darwinian natural selection.[52]
Richard Dawkins

Then God said, "Let us make man in our image, after our likeness."
Genesis 1:26

THE LIE IN THE CULTURE

With publication of his seminal work, *On the Origin of Species* (1859), naturalist Charles Darwin offered a materialist explanation of life's origins through a process of unguided evolution. Darwin needed to address two basic questions to advance his theory: the origin of the first form of life (chemical evolution) and the origin of the abundant and diverse forms of life that now populate the earth (biological evolution). He has little to say about the origin of the first form of life, wishing in an 1871 letter to Joseph Hooker: "But if (and oh what a big if) we could conceive in some warm little pond with all sorts of ammonia and phosphoric salts, light, heat, electricity etcetera present, that a protein compound was chemically formed, ready to undergo still more complex changes."[53] The warm little pond has eluded discovery.

---

[52] Richard Dawkins. *The God Delusion* (New York: Harper Collins, 2008), 24.

Darwin devoted his energies more enthusiastically to biological evolution, proposing the theory of common descent: "We must likewise admit that all the organic beings which have ever lived on this earth may be descended from some one primordial form."[54] According to this view, a single, universal ancestor gave rise to all forms of life today, from the lowly ant to the ponderous elephant, the tenacious weed to the mighty oak, the single-celled bacterium to the enormous gray whale. All forms of life are lineally connected to the same, original ancestor. Darwin conceptualized this interrelatedness in a tree of life, with numerous branches radiating from a central, earlier trunk. He ultimately published a separate volume, *The Descent of Man* (1871), to extend the notion of common descent to nature's highest achievement, mankind.

> Man with all his noble qualities, with sympathy which feels for the most debased, with benevolence which extends not only to other men but to the humblest living creature, with his god-like intellect which has penetrated into the movements and constitution of the solar system—with all these exalted powers— Man still bears in his bodily frame the indelible stamp of his lowly origin.[55]

The postulated mechanisms for the alleged achievements of evolution, including human evolution, have changed little since their conception. Built on Darwin's then understanding of genetics, variation, and modification, the prevailing neo-Darwinian theory can be summarized in this triad:

1. Evolutionary change occurs as the result of random, minute variations, or mutations.
2. The process of natural selection sifts among these to preserve variations that confer survival advantage or enhance fitness.

---

[53] Lucas Brouwers. "Did Life Evolve in a 'Warm Little Pond'?" *Scientific American* (Feb. 16, 2012). https://tinyurl.com/xvhcpj7e.
[54] Charles Darwin. *The Origin of Species* (New York: Penguin Group, 1958), 502.
[55] Charles Darwin. *The Descent of Man* (Delhi: Open Books, 2020), Loc 11178, Kindle.

3. Favored variations are inherited and spread in subsequent generations.

It was not until Francis Crick and James Watson co-discovered the double-helix structure of DNA in 1953 that the precise mechanisms of mutation and inheritance were fully understood. Nonetheless, the essential features of Darwin's original theory remain intact.

This mechanistic triad, no matter how elegantly described, comes down to mindless, unguided chance. Random mutations are just that, random. There is no wisdom or plan, no insight or design, no mind or purpose. At its root, evolutionary theory is materialistic and atheistic. It does not invite nor require God's involvement. Its adherents embrace a form of circular reasoning: if evolution is true, there is no God; if there is no God, evolution must be true. Evolutionary theory was atheistic in its conception and is atheistic in its continued progress. Of Thomas Huxley, a friend of Darwin and early convert to Darwinism, Tom Wolfe states, "Huxley became such an ardent Darwinist not because he believed in Darwin's theory of natural selection—he never did—but because Darwin was obviously an atheist, just as he was."[56]

History supports the connection of evolutionism to atheism. The twentieth century saw the emergence of new totalitarian political ideologies that were grounded in scientific materialism, atheism, and evolutionism, among them communism and national socialism. Communism then and now holds sway over a significant proportion of the world's population. Closer to home, 65 percent of self-described atheists in the U.S. and 43 percent of self-described agnostics believe that "the findings of science make the existence of God less probable," citing two scientific ideas as most influential in the loss of faith: unguided chemical evolution and unguided biological evolution.[57]

In its materialistic and atheistic essence, evolution is the orthodoxy of the secular academy. Few express this better than Richard Dawkins, who holds to the articles of evolutionary faith with a religious zeal: "It

---

[56] Tom Wolfe. *The Kingdom of Speech* (New York: Hachette Book Group, 2016), 48.

[57] John G. West. "Darwin's Corrosive Idea: The Impact of Evolution on Attitudes About Faith, Ethics, and Human Uniqueness." *Discovery Institute* (2016), 1-4. https://tinyurl.com/5azk8emw.

is absolutely safe to say that if you meet somebody who claims not to believe in evolution, that person is ignorant, stupid or insane."[58] One admires Dawkins' uncompromising consistency with his belief system, which is more than can be said for many theists. Evolutionary passion is expressed more lyrically by Stephen Baird, a colleague of mine at the University of California, San Diego. A physician-scientist turned singer-songwriter, Baird leads the Galapagos Mountain Boys and is the creative force behind their "scientific gospel music." Raised in the Bible Belt, Baird converted to rationalism as a student at Stanford University. Now he parodies Christian music with album titles such as *Hallelujah! Evolution!* or *Ain't Gonna Be No Judgment Day*.[59] Baird seeks to convince minds while appealing to hearts. With other new atheists like Dawkins, he is succeeding.

THE LIE IN THE CHURCH

Lest you think you need to look long for "scientific gospel music" and melodies extolling evolution, not to worry. Just tune in Hillsong United to hear this similar refrain:

And as You speak
A hundred billion creatures catch Your breath
Evolving in pursuit of what You said
If it all reveals Your nature so will I[60]

To be fair, Hillsong United takes it to the next level, with a professional band, techie stage lighting, fog machines, and huge crowds. But the slick performance cannot mask the lie of the lyrics: we are evolving. Stephen Baird would be envious; Charles Darwin would be pleased.

Joel Houston, son of Hillsong's cofounder, confirmed the lie when asked about the meaning of these lyrics: "Evolution is undeniable—created by God as a reflective means of displaying nature's pattern of

---

[58] Richard Dawkins. "Book Review: Solving the Mystery of Evolution." *New York Times* (Apr. 9, 1989).

[59] Stephen Baird. https://en.wikipedia.org/wiki/Stephen_Baird.

[60] Hillsong United. "So Will I (100 Billion X)." https://tinyurl.com/2sm8hmky.

renewal in pursuance of God's Word."[61] Houston's defense of "So Will I" signals the growing acceptance of evolution in the church. Rebranded as "theistic evolution" or, less commonly, "evolutionary creationism," neo-Darwinian evolution is accepted by both historic and evangelical American denominations. What is embraced is not theistic at all, since the neo-Darwinian tenets of atheistic, evolutionary orthodoxy are fully conserved. It is an unworkable and untenable hybrid of the sacred and the secular. It is the new syncretism. Religious syncretism did not work during the times of the Old Testament, when the kings of Israel and Judah attempted to blend pagan idolatry with the worship of the Hebrew God. The latter invariably lost out, precipitating God's eventual judgment of both nations at the hands of Assyria and Babylonia, respectively. Syncretism does not work today. Theism and evolutionism are as incompatible now as the worship of Yahweh and Baal in the eighth century BC. For this reason, I will henceforth simply speak of "evolution" or "evolutionary theory" or "evolutionism" when discussing the dynamics within the church, since "theistic evolution" is self-contradicting. Such linguistic misdirection is a common progressive tactic to breed confusion and conceal the truth. "Theistic evolution" makes no more sense than "theistic materialism" or, for that matter, "theistic atheism." On this, Dawkins and I agree. In his words, so-called theistic evolutionists are "deluded" in their efforts "to smuggle God in the back door."[62]

How widespread is the lie in the church? Researchers at the Massachusetts Institute of Technology surveyed Americans in 2013 on religious attitudes and beliefs regarding origins. They observed that a mere 11 percent of respondents belonged to religious traditions that openly reject evolution.[63] This means that almost 90 percent of Americans either belong to a religious tradition that accepts evolution or do not belong to a religious tradition at all. An earlier analysis in

---

[61] Jeannie Ortega Law. "Hillsong's Joel Houston Clarifies Evolution Views After Sparking Debate with Worship Song 'So Will I.'" *Christian Post* (Jun. 29, 2018). https://tinyurl.com/krvh2564.

[62] John Farrell. "It's Time to Retire 'Theistic Evolution.'" *Forbes* (Mar. 9, 2016). https://tinyurl.com/2p9ct6ue.

[63] Eugena Lee et al. "The MIT Survey on Science, Religion and Origins: The Belief Gap." https://tinyurl.com/3ctd8x5z.

2010 by Joel Martin, a Presbyterian evolutionist at the Natural History Museum of Los Angeles County, summarizes the positions on evolution of major Christian denominations, corroborating that "there is more acceptance than non-acceptance of evolution among Christians, based on statements from their organizing bodies or spokespersons."[64] He estimates a greater than 2:1 ratio of adherents in evolution-accepting versus non-accepting denominations (94 million versus 46 million). The evolution-accepting denominations or organizations include Roman Catholic, United Methodist, Evangelical Lutheran Church in America, African Methodist Episcopal Church, Presbyterian Church (USA), Episcopal Church, Greek Orthodox Archdiocese of America, and United Church of Christ. The minority, evolution-rejecting denominations or organizations include the Southern Baptist Convention, National Baptist Convention USA, Church of God in Christ, International Circle of Faith, Calvary Chapel, Church of God (Cleveland), Assemblies of God, Lutheran Church–Missouri Synod, Seventh-Day Adventists, International Church of the Foursquare Gospel, and New Apostolic Church. The lie is well circulated in the historic church and spreading fast.

Masked by both analyses are internal divisions within the more conservative traditions categorized by Martin as non-accepting of evolution. A case in point is the Assemblies of God. At the time of Martin's research, the Assemblies of God's "doctrine of creation" (1977) was unambiguous in its rejection of evolution. When the MIT researchers performed their survey in 2013, the Assemblies of God was reclassified as evolution-affirming in view of a new, "conciliatory" position statement approved in 2010, from which they quote, "The Bible makes no claim to be a scientific textbook, nor should it be understood as such."[65] The researchers also highlight the opinion of two evolution-affirming academics, whose *A Brief Overview of Pentecostal Views on Origins* was published in the denomination's *Enrichment Journal* in 2010, also quoting them, "Pentecostal Christians do not

---

[64] Joel W. Martin. "Compatibility of Major U.S. Christian Denominations with Evolution." *Evolution: Education and Outreach* (2010), 420-431.

[65] Lee, *The MIT Survey on Science, Religion, and Origins*, 22.

share a single viewpoint on evolution. Pentecostals concur that God exists and is the Creator, but they do not speak with one voice on how ancient creation is, how much evolution has occurred, or whether science provides evidence for an intelligent designer."[66]

What led this conservative, Pentecostal denomination to engage in the century-old fundamentalist-modernist controversy on the side of the modernists? Leaders were aware of the growing acceptance of evolution within the denomination. A 2010 survey of faculty and students at Assemblies of God colleges and universities showed that 16 percent accepted evolution as a biblical explanation of origins. (A more rigorous Pew Research Center study [2007 to 2014] showed that 33 percent of Pentecostals believe in evolution).[67] The 2010 doctrinal compromise, approved by its governing General Presbytery, appears to have gained early support from the executive leadership of the denomination and key faculty at its academic flagship, Evangel University. This opened the door to the inaugural *Faith and Science* conference held in 2011 at Evangel University; academics were organizing and convening with the visible support of the denomination's executive leadership. Evolutionary perspectives were cordially included, not for the purpose of understanding viewpoints in conflict with Scripture but of accepting them as within the boundaries of biblical orthodoxy. Pentecostal scholar and evolutionist Amos Yong celebrated the fact that the 2010 doctrinal revision "creates space for the many scientists and theologians who teach in the fellowship's colleges and universities to explore various theories of creation," empowering "the scientific and theological search for the truth."[68] The story does not end there, however. A grass roots reaction led to a correction of the Doctrine of Creation position in 2014 that upheld the biblical doctrine of the special creation of Adam and disallowed evolutionism.[69] It

---

[66] Mike Tenneson and Steve Badger. "A Brief Overview of Pentecostal Views on Origins." *Enrichment Journal* (2010). https://tinyurl.com/bdftvs2v.

[67] "Religious Landscape Study: Views About Human Evolution Among Pentecostals in the Evangelical Tradition." *Pew Research Center.* https://tinyurl.com/2xmx88au.

[68] Amos Yong. "Pentecostalism and Science: Challenges and Opportunities." *Proceedings of the Inaugural Faith & Science Conference* (2011), 137.

[69] Doctrine of Creation, Assemblies of God. https://tinyurl.com/sxxanta6.

remains to be seen if this will arrest the spread of the lie of man's common descent within the Assemblies of God.

No one has done more to advance evolution in the evangelical wing of the American church than BioLogos, promoting evolution to Christian denominations as well as Christian educational institutions. Founded by physician-scientist Francis Collins, who rose to prominence for his research on the human genome and as Director of the National Institute of Health, BioLogos has popularized the evolution branded by his influential book, *The Language of God*. Collins affirms there is "still the possibility of a richly satisfying harmony between the scientific and spiritual worldviews" in this "modern era of cosmology, evolution, and the human genome."[70] BioLogos' statement of beliefs reflects a similar understanding.

> We believe that the diversity and interrelation of all life on earth are best explained by the God-ordained process of evolution with common descent. Thus, evolution is not in opposition to God, but a means by which God providentially achieves his purposes. Therefore, we reject ideologies that claim that evolution is a purposeless process or that evolution replaces God. We believe that God created humans in biological continuity with all life on earth, but also as spiritual beings. God established a unique relationship with humanity by endowing us with his image and calling us to an elevated position within the created order.[71]

This framework conserves the core doctrines of neo-Darwinian evolution, including the standard evolutionary mechanisms, evolution as a random, unguided process (except for initial conditions), and universal common descent as the evolutionary explanation for all life forms, including man. It conserves the essential tenet of secular science, "theological naturalism": "the primary theological ground rule is that scientific explanations must be naturalistic."[72] Scientism thrives in this

---

[70] Francis S. Collins. *The Language of God: A Scientist Presents Evidence for Belief* (New York: Simon & Schuster, 2006), 5.

[71] BioLogos. "What We Believe." https://tinyurl.com/3bvu986a.

[72] Cornelius Hunter. *Science's Blind Spot: The Unseen Religion of Scientific Naturalism*

framework while Scripture suffers, with little patience for either the supernatural content or the historical meaning of Genesis. Steve Fuller rightly observes, "The charge laid at the doorstep of theistic evolutionists is that the doorstep is exactly where they leave their religious commitments when they enter the house of science."[73]

The reason for this separation is the "evolutionary hermeneutic" employed by BioLogos. Theologian Wayne Grudem outlines its devastating impact upon biblical doctrine:

1. Genesis 1-3 is not a historical narrative that reports events that happened.
2. God was the Creator of matter, not of living creatures.
3. There were not merely two but thousands of ancestors of humans.
4. Adam and Eve (if they existed) were born of human parents, were not the first humans, and were not specially created.
5. Adam and Eve (if they existed) were never sinless; their sin did not bring about physical death.
6. God did not create animal life, did not create a "very good world," did not rest from his work, and did not place a curse on the creation.[74]

This diminished view of Scripture opens the floodgates to other compromises. Historic denominations (Evangelical Church of North America; Presbyterian Church (USA); United Methodist Church) departed down the path of compromise with evolution long before BioLogos even existed. This has led to their widespread embrace of other progressive lies such as abortion, homosexuality, transgenderism, and critical theory, which are the subjects of upcoming chapters. BioLogos' constituents appear to be on the same course, among them progressives highlighted in the preceding chapter, Peter Enns and Ken

---

(Grand Rapids, Michigan: Brazos Press, 2007), 11.

[73] Steve Fuller. "Foreword." In *Theistic Evolution: A Scientific, Philosophical, and Theological Critique*, edited by J. P. Moreland et al (Wheaton, Illinois: Crossway, 2017), 28.

[74] Wayne Grudem. "Biblical and Theological Introduction to Theistic Evolution." In *Theistic Evolution*, Moreland et al, 61-71.

Wilson. Both have collaborated with BioLogos to promote its evolutionary premises but have not been content to stop there, moving on to press other progressive, nonbiblical, and unorthodox positions. Amos Yong was a member of the BioLogos Advisory Council when he championed his denomination's 2010 doctrinal concession to evolution. He has made his own politically correct concessions since, including misgendering the Holy Spirit as "she,"[75] racializing modern missions for spreading "the 'white' gospel," [76] and promoting woke sensitivity to "demonizing human others: those of other ethnicities, languages, cultures, (dis)abilities, and even religious traditions and sexual orientations."[77] This progression is mirrored in the teachings of megachurch pastor Andy Stanley, who accepts evolution ("there's no necessary conflict between Theism and Evolution"[78]), discounts the authority of the Bible (the Old Testament should not be "the go-to source regarding any behavior in the church"[79]), and speaks ambiguously, if not affirmingly, of homosexuality.[80] Compromise of the foundational truths of Genesis invariably invites compromise of downstream biblical truths, shredding the authority of Scripture. While many within the church continue the futile effort to couple evolutionism and biblicism, others have realized their inherent incompatibility and quit on faith altogether. Their deconversion stories are poignant and tragic.

A treasure on my bookshelf is an autographed hardcover edition of Billy Graham's autobiography *Just as I Am*. It chronicles the journey of the twentieth century's greatest evangelist. It also casts a long shadow on the memory of Graham's contemporary and friend, Charles Templeton. Templeton's relationship with Graham solidified when they

---

[75] Amos Yong. *Mission After Pentecost: The Witness of the Spirit from Genesis to Revelation* (Grand Rapids, Michigan: Baker Academic, 2019), 191.

[76] Yong, *Mission After Pentecost*, 283.

[77] Yong, *Mission After Pentecost*, 274.

[78] "Andy Stanley Denies the Creation Account in Genesis, Apparently He Knows Better Than God." *The Dissenter* (Apr. 11, 2023). https://tinyurl.com/ypvnb62w.

[79] Albert Mohler. "Getting 'Unhitched' from the Old Testament? Andy Stanley Aims at Heresy." *Albert Mohler* (Aug. 10, 2018). https://tinyurl.com/2s4jnkty.

[80] Andrew Marin. "Andy Stanley, Al Mohler, and Homosexuality." *Christianity Today* (May 8, 2012). https://tinyurl.com/465krn2f.

roomed and ministered together during a 1946 Youth for Christ evangelistic tour of Europe. However, in less than a decade, Templeton would declare himself an agnostic. Templeton's problems with God began with his problems with Genesis. In his 1996 memoir *Farewell to God*, he underscores his evolutionary skepticism of the Genesis account of Adam's special creation among the reasons for his crisis of faith.[81] For Templeton, it was indisputable that "all life is the result of timeless evolutionary forces."[82] Shortly before his death in 2001, he gave an interview to Lee Strobel, a copy of Graham's *Just as I Am* at his side. Though fixed in his unbelief and agnosticism, Templeton would conclude the interview with tearful ambivalence when discussing his separation from Jesus: "In my view, he is the most important human being who has ever existed. And if I may put it this way, *I ... miss ... him!*"[83]

In 1995, while visiting Cambridge, England, I heard an example of the very finest in exegetical preaching in a message by Roy Clements drawn from John's first epistle. An audience primarily of students from the nearby University of Cambridge eagerly received it. Then pastor of Eden Baptist Church, Clements was highly regarded for his biblical exposition by none other than John Stott, who was also his good friend. However, in 1999, he would resign from pastoral ministry and leave his wife and four children to begin a relationship with another man. What went wrong? Like Templeton, Clements' crisis of faith is traceable to doubts of the Bible, including "creation/evolution." In a 1999 letter to Stott, Clements echoes the sentiments of Peter Enns: "Some obscurantists refuse to admit the influence of extra-biblical knowledge and experience upon biblical interpretation. But such influence is both inevitable and necessary. Thus, 7-day creationists shut their eyes to the scientific evidence insisting their interpretation of Genesis 1 is self-evidently right."[84]

---

[81] Charles Templeton. *Farewell to God* (Ontario, Canada: McClelland & Stewart, 1996), 30.
[82] Templeton, *Farewell to God*, 232.
[83] Lee Strobel. *The Case for Faith* (Grand Rapids, Michigan: Zondervan, 2021), 14.
[84] Roy Clements. "A Letter to an Old Friend." https://tinyurl.com/46h7mdju.

More recently, social influencer Rhett McLaughlin published the story of his fall from faith on the popular Rhett & Link YouTube channel. Entitled *Rhett's Spiritual Deconstruction*, the episode has been viewed by millions. His story begins as a childhood friend of "Link" Neal, with whom he enjoyed a strong Christian bond that continued into college. During their initial careers as engineers, Rhett and Link produced video content for Cru (formerly Campus Crusade for Christ), eventually joining Cru in full-time ministry positions. Their media talents led them to leave ministry, move to Los Angeles, and devote their efforts to their YouTube channel, which has been highly popular. Their business success paralleled their spiritual decline. McLaughlin describes a key turning point in his 2020 YouTube video.

> Then in 2006, I read a book called *The Language of God* by Francis Collins. This is the kind of thing that I lived for. I loved it when someone who was a scientific mind, who was respected by the world, would come out and basically do this, make it reasonable to be a Christian, to show you that your faith was reasonable and smart people believed this … Collins starts talking about the undeniable evidence for evolution, evidence that humans evolved from a common ancestor with apes. And I was like hold up y'all. What? This guy's a Christian? I know that's not true … Essentially, every criticism of evolution that I held [to] justify my unwillingness to believe in it turned out to be a misconception or a misrepresentation of the facts. And so after reading a bunch of books, talking to a lot of people—now listen, I didn't wanna believe this. I'd spent my whole life not believing this and not wanting to believe this, but I kind of was just faced with this, that evolution was by far the best explanation for what we actually see in the real world.[85]

Flipped from his biblical position by the evolutionary views of Collins, does McLaughlin stop there? He cannot. He draws an analogy to tugging on a thread in his "sweater of faith" which is successively

---

[85] Rhett McLaughlin. "Rhett's Spiritual Deconstruction." https://tinyurl.com/fwcc74zr.

reduced to a vest, then a midriff, then a halter top, then a bikini top, at which point it is useless. Quoting from his personal journal, he ends this way: "I don't think it insignificant that the deeper I have dug into Christianity with a thirst for the truth, the more difficult it has become to have faith. In fact, for me, it has become impossible."

Sadly, the stories of lost faith under the spell of evolution are more the rule than the exception, as the string of chilling comments below McLaughlin's YouTube video testify. They support theologian J.P. Moreland's assessment: "In my view, there are certain contemporary currents of thought that risk undercutting Christianity as a source of knowledge, and I shall argue that by its very nature, theistic evolution is the prime culprit. It is one of the church's leading gravediggers."[86]

If Darwin and Dawkins are right in their assertion that man is commonly descended from a single, universal ancestor, or if Collins is right that man is the product of random neo-Darwinian evolution rather than God's special creation, then the veracity of the Bible is very much in question as is its usefulness as a source of any meaningful knowledge. There would be no compelling reason *not* to follow the examples of Templeton, Clements, or McLaughlin. But they are lying.

THE BIBLICAL TRUTH

In response to these narratives, allow me to recount my own journey, which is quite different—and more hopeful—in its outcome. As a teenager, I read Darwin's *On the Origin of Species* and *The Descent of Man* in order to understand better the prevailing faith of the culture, though antithetical to my own. I knew the mechanisms and implications of neo-Darwinian evolution, and I was aware of efforts to harmonize—or syncretize—this with Scripture. Why did I reject evolution? First, it lacks face validity. I look at my left hand (I am left-handed and a violinist) and am amazed by its design. I know that the execution of a composition by Mozart or Paganini requires a complex series of steps

---

[86] J.P. Moreland. "How Theistic Evolution Kicks Christianity Out of the Plausibility Structure and Robs Christians of Confidence that the Bible Is a Source of Knowledge." In *Theistic Evolution*, Moreland et al, 638.

that occur instantaneously, originating in the brain to direct the playing of a musical passage with the required intonation, rhythm, and tone. Neuronal signals move down axons and across synapses through complex chemical reactions along delicate cellular membranes, reaching target motor cells that coordinate the fine and balancing movements of flexor and extensor tendons to guide the fingers in the desired way, with real-time sensory feedback sent back to the brain through highly sensitive pathways originating in the ends of each digit. I more fully grasped the amazing anatomy of my hand when I underwent a flexor tenosynovectomy, an open surgery on my left index finger in 2020, seeing for the first time the inside of my finger. Neither this surgery nor time have dissuaded me of this conviction as I observe the world around me in its manifold splendor. This was the intuition of the Psalmist, who three thousand years ago recognized that he was "fearfully and wonderfully made."[87] Random, unguided mutations are insufficient.

However, that is not *the* reason for me. *The* reason is that the Bible is true. And, unlike neo-Darwinian evolution, the Bible has face validity. Yes, it is received by faith. But it reasonably explains the wonders of creation, addresses the spiritual needs of man, and rests on the reliable testimony of the Son, whom God raised from the dead. I accept the Word of God as a whole; the Creator and the Son are one. If my faith is misplaced, then there is no other explanation for the cosmos or for biology than some impersonal, protracted process of trial and error. I would have no reason *not* to be a scientific materialist and atheist. If I am deceived either in my assessment of the world around me or in my confidence in Scripture, then I would be the first to join the Apostle Paul in obeying the ancient imperative of the hopeless: "Let us eat and drink, for tomorrow we die."[88] Instead, I am confident in my hope in Christ, who made me and who saved me. The Bible is true.

Just as the Bible extols Christ as Creator of the universe, so it also extols him as Creator of life. "For his invisible attributes, namely, his eternal power and divine nature, have been clearly perceived, ever since

---

[87] Psalm 139:14.
[88] 1 Corinthians 15:32.

the creation of the world, in the things that have been made. So they are without excuse."[89] This understanding was affirmed in the early creeds of the church, including the First Council of Nicaea (325 AD): "We believe in one God, the Father Almighty, Maker of all things visible and invisible. And in one Lord Jesus Christ, the Son of God ... by whom all things were made, both in heaven and on earth."[90] This is why devoted evolutionists place "Darwin fish" emblems on their car bumpers, substituting IXTHUS (the first Greek letters of the words *Jesus Christ, God's Son, Savior*) from the early Christian fish symbol with DARWIN. It is all about Jesus' Lordship as Creator, which evolution seeks to steal.

The central biological theme of Genesis is the creation of man, in keeping with the overall trajectory of Scripture. The first chapter of Genesis summarizes man's origin this way: "Then God said, 'Let us make man in our image, after our likeness.'"[91] This verse tells us that man was created by God through the power of his Word, not evolved over millions of years from a single common ancestor. Importantly, man is made in the image of God (*imago dei*), conferring upon him the unique quality of God's likeness. This imparts to every person an unconditional value that cannot be overestimated but which is erased by evolutionary theory.

Man in God's image supports not only his exceptionalism but also his essentialism, the notion that man has fixed attributes that are necessary—or essential—to his identity. Human speciation distinct from any other animal life, humanity as male and female, and man's capacity for fellowship with God are among these attributes. These attributes do not evolve or change. Man's essential nature—spiritually, psychologically, emotionally, and physically—is static and immutable. This distinguishes the Genesis account from the evolutionary view, which is progressive in its view that everything is in flux.

Scripture teaches the historicity of Adam. Genesis includes a seamless genealogy from Adam to the captivity in Egypt at the time of

---

[89] Romans 1:20.
[90] The Creed of Nicaea. https://tinyurl.com/259cyx7t.
[91] Genesis 1:26.

Abraham's grandson, Jacob, and great grandson, Joseph. The historical book of first Chronicles begins with one word: "Adam."[92] Perhaps no people has excelled in such record keeping as the Jewish people. Accurate genealogies were vital to preserving their identity across the millennia. Further, their understanding of God is rooted in the objective history of God's relationships to real people who lived in real places at real times. Genealogical precision was vital. Together with a plain reading of the creation narrative, these genealogies point to a recent beginning of human history.

Support for a historical Adam also comes from the New Testament. In his Gospel, physician and historian Luke traces the human lineage of Jesus through Mary, "being the son (as was supposed) of Joseph," directly to the earliest patriarchs previously recounted by Moses in Genesis:

> ... the son of Judah, the son of Jacob, the son of Isaac, the son of Abraham, the son of Terah, the son of Nahor, the son of Serug, the son of Reu, the son of Peleg, the son of Eber, the son of Shelah, the son of Cainan, the son of Arphaxad, the son of Shem, the son of Noah, the son of Lamech, the son of Methuselah, the son of Enoch, the son of Jared, the son of Mahalaleel, the son of Cainan, the son of Enos, the son of Seth, the son of Adam, the son of God.[93]

Jesus himself refers to Adam and Eve when he quotes from Genesis in response to the Pharisees: "Have you not read that he who created them from the beginning made them male and female, and said, 'Therefore a man shall leave his father and his mother and hold fast to his wife, and the two shall become one flesh?'"[94] On multiple occasions, the Apostle Paul builds his Christology on the correspondence and contrast between the first Adam and the second

---

[92] 1 Chronicles 1:1.
[93] Luke 3:23, 33-37.
[94] Matthew 19:3-5.

Adam, Jesus: "The first man was from the earth, a man of dust; the second man is from heaven."[95]

The biblical doctrine of Adam goes beyond Adam's historical significance as the father of humanity. It also encompasses his original sin (*peccatum originis*), which introduced death, disease, and suffering to all of humanity and all of nature. Every person shares the image of God but also the mark of Adam's sin. This is the problem that the balance of Scripture addresses. Genesis 3 offers an early prophetic hint of its solution. Speaking to the serpent after his temptation of Adam and Eve, God says, "I will put enmity between you and the woman, and between your offspring and her offspring; he shall bruise your head, and you shall bruise his heel."[96] This is the vital link between the Fall and the Cross. The sin of the first Adam would be addressed by the offspring of the woman, Jesus, who, on the Cross, would atone for man's sin and strike a crushing blow to the serpent's head. Paul explains this in his letter to the Romans: "For if, because of one man's trespass, death reigned through that one man, much more will those who receive the abundance of grace and the free gift of righteousness reign in life through the one man Jesus Christ."[97]

The existence of a historical Adam is fundamental to the twin biblical doctrines of the special creation of man and the Fall of man; both justify the redemptive plan that unfolds across Scripture, culminating in the atoning death and resurrection of Christ. This is an immense problem for BioLogos-style evolutionists who attempt to insinuate Darwinism into Genesis. Even Rhett McLaughlin worried about this very point before succumbing to evolutionary dogma: "What I knew is that Adam and Eve had to be real. Adam and Eve had to be real because so much comes from them being real. That's the Fall, that's where the Fall happens, and the Fall is the reason that we have original sin, and original sin is why we need a Savior."[98] McLaughlin is right. Once he had assented to the evolutionary doctrine of common

---

[95] 1 Corinthians 15:47.
[96] Genesis 3:14.
[97] Romans 5:17.
[98] McLaughlin, *Rhett's Spiritual Deconstruction*.

descent, he had no choice but to abandon his belief in a historical Adam and ultimately his faith in Christ.

McLaughlin's deadly intuition is echoed by Quaker minister Philip Gulley, who rejects the Genesis creation narrative, the historicity of Adam, and, inevitably, the doctrine of original sin, concluding, "Any God who would condemn billions of people to hell because the first couple sampled a bit of fruit seems at the very least eccentric, and at worst despotic."[99] Gulley urges the church to revamp its approach to Scripture, reimagine the life of Jesus, and replace guilt-ridden hymns like *Amazing Grace* with progressive and permissive ones that reflect "God's inclusive love."[100]

BioLogos' position on the matter is similarly compromising. Like Gulley's, it takes the claims of science very seriously but at the expense of the doctrine of salvation taught by Moses, demonstrated by Jesus, and explained by the Apostles. It is dictated by the same data used by others to support atheistic evolution, giving credence to the latest scientific literature but discounting the enduring witness of Scripture.

> At BioLogos, we are persuaded by the scientific evidence that *Homo sapiens* evolved, arising about 200,000 years ago and sharing common ancestors with all other life on Earth … The genetic diversity among humans today could not have come from just two *Homo sapiens* individuals, but a population of thousands. Traditional interpretations of Scripture should not be lightly dismissed, but neither is it responsible to ignore or dismiss the results of scientific inquiry simply because they conflict with traditional interpretations.[101]

The existence or non-existence of a supernaturally created, historic Adam is the crux of the matter. If there is no first Adam, there can be no second Adam. If there is no Fall, there is no need for a Savior. If death and struggle drove the evolutionary progress that resulted in

---

[99] Philip Gulley. *If the Church Were Christian: Rediscovering the Values of Jesus* (New York, NY: HarperCollins, 2009), 31.
[100] Gulley, *If the Church Were Christian*, 34.
[101] BioLogos. "Common Questions." https://tinyurl.com/hbyebe25.

humankind, the narrative of Genesis is a fiction, a misleading fabrication. If the understanding of Genesis' opening chapters upheld by Jesus, the Apostles, and the early church is wrong, Christian doctrine is a shambles. There is no common ground between a specially and supernaturally created Adam and evolution's cardinal doctrine of common descent. This was the basis of the corrective wording inserted into the revised, 2014 Assemblies of God Doctrine of Creation position: "Both Adam and Eve, male and female, are declared to be made in the 'image' and 'likeness' of God ... Any evolutionary theory, including theistic evolution/evolutionary creationism, that claims all forms of life arose from a common ancestry is thereby ruled out."[102] Even Tim Keller, a BioLogos ally, draws the line at this point.

> Before God I'm trying my best to read this as I think what the Scripture says. Right now, it says to me, you know, there is an Adam and Eve, and everyone came from Adam and Eve, and they were a special creation, and so even though I don't have an answer to my scientist friends, that is where I stand."[103]

In his recent book, *The Genealogical Adam & Eve: The Surprising Science of Universal Ancestry*, physician-scientist and computational biologist S. Joshua Swamidass explores a speculative workaround to this problem. He affirms the traditional understanding of Genesis that "Adam and Eve were real people who 1) lived in the Middle East, just several thousand years ago; 2) were the ancestors of everyone; and 3) were created, with no parents, by a direct act of God."[104] He bridges the impasse with evolution by distinguishing between genealogical ancestry and genetic ancestry. The first, our lineal connection to, say Adam and Eve, could be intact but with no genetic trace. Thus, scientifically, all people currently living could be lineally descended from Adam and Eve, who could have been specially created and placed in the Garden of

---

[102] Doctrine of Creation, Assemblies of God. https://tinyurl.com/4sn33sca.

[103] Timothy Keller et al. "Keller, Moore, and Duncan on the Non-Negotiable Beliefs About Creation." *The Gospel Coalition* (Aug. 29, 2017). https://tinyurl.com/2vhpjvu9.

[104] S. Joshua Swamidass. *The Genealogical Adam & Eve: The Surprising Science of Universal Ancestry* (Downers Grove, Illinois: InterVarsity, 2019), 5.

Eden. But what about evolution and common descent? Swamidass also believes that a large community of evolved, human-like creatures existed outside of the Garden. Once Adam and Eve were expelled, there would have been interbreeding, explaining the genetic diversity presently observed. In the end, the human genome reflects common descent. This solution is void of biblical support, however, and leaves unanswered the same critical questions of original sin, death, and salvation avoided by BioLogos.

Are the claims of evolution so compelling as to require this novel though unsupported compromise? Does nature speak of the special creation of man, or does it tell of his gradual, imperceptible evolution over millions of years? First, let me return to the idea of face validity, which I previously cited as personally compelling. It does not take a doctorate in molecular biology, genetics, or anatomy to recognize design behind the complexity and diversity of life. It is self-evident. This was decisive for American Communist and atheist Whittaker Chamber's rejection of evolution, occurring in an unguarded moment while marveling at the beauty of his beloved only child.

> My eye came to rest on the intricate convolutions of her ear—those intricate, perfect ears. The thought passed through my mind: "No, those ears were not created by any chance coming together of atoms in nature (the Communist view). They could have been created only by immense design." The thought was involuntary and unwanted. I crowded it out of my mind. But I never wholly forgot it or the occasion. I had to crowd it out of my mind. If I had completed it, I should have to say: Design presupposes God. I did not then know that, at that moment, the finger of God was first laid on my forehead.[105]

The finger of God that rested on Chamber's forehead touches everything around us. The first imprint of God's finger of design is the rich substrate of information, of language, that informs all of biology. Each living cell operates according to a highly specified language in the

---

[105] Whittaker Chambers. *Witness* (Washington DC: Regnery History, 1952), 705.

same way a computer operates according to written code. This language is not a series of 0's and 1's as in computer programs but rather a four-letter code determined by nucleobases (symbolized as C, T, A, G). Arrangements of these bases in DNA correspond to amino acids, which form proteins. Proteins are the building blocks for higher levels of organization, leading ultimately to intracellular organelles, cells, tissues, organs, and organisms. The human genome is three billion letters long and contains all the information needed to build a complex, fully functioning human being. If read at a rate of one letter per second, it would take thirty-one years to peruse it in its entirety.[106]

During my undergraduate years, I worked in a neuropharmacology lab at the Salk Institute, performing tasks in support of research on fetal alcohol syndrome. The Salk Institute rests atop the bluffs of La Jolla, California, overlooking the Pacific Ocean. The Institute is as picturesque as it is historic. While having lunch one day in the cafeteria, I noticed the Institute's namesake, Jonas Salk, sitting at an adjacent table. Salk is a household name for his groundbreaking discovery of the polio vaccine. Seated with him was none other than Francis Crick, mentioned earlier for his co-discovery of DNA in 1953, for which he, along with James Watson, would receive the 1962 Nobel Prize in Physiology or Medicine. Crick wondered how this universal genetic code came about in the first place. He faced the biological equivalent of the something-from-nothing problem that confounds cosmologists: how can brilliant code arise from chaos? In a 1973 article with Salk Institute's Leslie Orgel, Crick proposed a solution, directed panspermia, "the theory that organisms were directly transmitted to the earth by intelligent beings on another planet."[107] Crick's implausible theory misses the obvious: the finger of God.

Since the purpose of DNA is to specify proteins, and since proteins are the building blocks upon which biological systems are built, how likely are functional proteins to arise by chance? Each protein consists of a string of amino acids, the sequence of which determines its function and the way it ultimately folds into its final three-dimensional

---

[106] Collins, *Language of God*, 1.
[107] F.H.C. Crick and L.E. Orgel. "Directed Panspermia." https://tinyurl.com/3xe6tura.

structure. Change an amino acid here or there and the protein is rendered useless. An analysis of a common enzyme, beta-lactamase, tested the relationship between the amino acid sequence and function. The investigator concludes that "the overall prevalence of sequences performing a specific function by any domain-sized fold may be as low as 1 in 10^{77}."[108] The likelihood of randomly generating the specific sequence of amino acids necessary for beta-lactamase function is as low as 1 in 100,000,000,000,000,000,000,000,000,000,000,000,000,000, 000,000,000,000,000,000,000,000,000,000,000. This approximates the number of atoms in the known universe. It is not just unlikely; it is impossible. Natural selection can only choose among randomly generated options, virtually all of which are gibberish. But things get worse for the neo-Darwinians. The problem is not just the improbability of functional proteins but the improbability of functional cells much less functional organisms. The information challenges only multiply.

Biology is more than just one protein, however improbable its occurrence may be, working in isolation. Each individual protein works in concert with other proteins in carefully calibrated and complex systems. The construction of each of the components of a system in sequence is improbable. But that is not the only problem. In many systems, *all* the components must be fully developed at the outset for the system to work. The whole system collapses if one component is missing or defective. Incremental changes through random mutations cannot accomplish such "irreducible complexity," a term coined by biochemist Michael Behe.[109] For irreducibly complex systems, it is all or nothing. An example of this is the human coagulation system. The circulatory system serves not only to deliver vital oxygen to tissues but also to prevent bleeding through pathways involving platelets and coagulation proteins. Coagulation proteins are many, operating in a finely tuned cascade to trigger the formation of protective clots. This life-saving system becomes deadly if just one component is altered or missing. Absence of factor VIII leads to hemophilia, a life-threatening

---

[108] Douglas D. Axe. "Estimating the Prevalence of Protein Sequences Adopting Functional Enzyme Folds." *Journal of Molecular Biology*, 341 (2004), 1295-315.

[109] Michael J. Behe. *Darwin's Black Box: The Biochemical Challenge to Evolution* (New York: Touchstone, 1996), 56.

bleeding disorder. Decreased anti-thrombin results in life-threatening blood clots. It is a marvelous system but works on a razor's edge between bleeding on the one hand and clotting on the other. It is irreducibly complex.

When stepping back further to the anatomy and behaviors of organisms, the mystery only deepens. In *Animal Algorithms*, Eric Cassell catalogues the extraordinary feats of insects with brains a fraction the size of higher animals. Honeybees work in a caste system to organize their labors, using sophisticated navigation and communication systems to locate their hives and track food sources. The three-thousand-mile migration to Mexico of monarch butterflies takes two or three generations to complete, yet the arriving descendent often settles on the same tree used by ancestral predecessors. Manufacturing protein silk with an elasticity and strength that defies human replication, spiders generate webs that are engineering masterpieces. Termites construct nests reaching as high as twenty feet with designated areas for nurseries, gardens, and waste disposal, cooled by a sophisticated ventilation system to assure stable, comfortable temperatures in a hot environment; this is all accomplished in the dark as termites cannot see! These astounding behaviors are innate, coded by genetic information that is transmitted reliably across generations.[110] They defy evolutionary explanation. They indicate instead the finger of God.

Equally elusive are evolutionary explanations for man's distinguishing faculty of speech. As early as 1772, with the publication of *Ueber den Ursprung der Sprache* (*On the Origin of Language*), Johann Gottfried Herder was confounded in his attempt to solve the puzzle of language in naturalistic terms.[111] Darwin picked up the effort in earnest but was similarly perplexed, unable to identify a shred of evidence for the evolution of human speech. Professional linguists have continued the futile search to the present with disappointing results. With other leading evolutionists, eminent linguist Noam Chomsky

---

[110] Eric Cassell. *Animal Algorithms: Evolution and the Mysterious Origin of Ingenious Instincts* (Seattle, Washington: Discovery Institute, 2021), 12-14.

[111] Neil Thomas. "Language: Darwin's Eternal Mystery." *Evolution News & Science Today* (Aug. 18, 2022). https://tinyurl.com/mrxubzp5.

concludes, "Based on the current state of evidence, we submit that the most fundamental questions about the origins and evolution of our linguistic capacity remain as mysterious as ever."[112] Author and journalist Tom Wolfe characterizes the significance of this concession in colorful terms, exploiting the power of rhetoric to put the matter to rest:

> It seems that eight heavy-weight Evolutionists—linguists, biologists, anthropologists, and computer scientists—had published an article announcing they were giving up, throwing in the towel, folding, crapping out when it came to the question of where speech—and language—comes from and how it works.[113]

Then there is the human mind, the human spirit, the human consciousness. This is the summit that exceeds the reach of the materialist. If matter is all that is, if man is the composite of so many atoms organized through an unguided evolutionary process, and if there is no God, what is the origin of the abiding sense of one's own significance, the powerful emotion of love, the deep pain of suffering, the longing for God, or the aspiration for eternity? If the materialists are right, humanity's sense of self-importance and worth is baseless and delusional. Alternatively, this sense may prove a spiritual essence endowed by the Creator in whose likeness man is made. "The spirit of man is the lamp of the Lord, searching all his innermost parts."[114] Philosopher and mathematician David Berlinski summarizes the state of the evidence this way:

> We do not have a serious scientific theory explaining the powers and properties of the human mind. The claim that the human mind is the product of evolution is not unassailable fact. It is barely coherent. The idea that man was created in the image of

---

[112] Marc D. Hauser, et al. "The Mystery of Language of Evolution." *Frontiers in Psychology* (May 7, 2014). https://tinyurl.com/2vvwaurf.

[113] Wolfe, *The Kingdom of Speech*, 3.

[114] Proverbs 20:27.

God remains what it has always been: And that is the instinctive default position of the human race.[115]

The common descent of man is as incoherent scientifically as it is theologically. Atheistic evolution falls on the sword of extreme—in truth impossible—improbability, while theistic evolution does so on the sword of biblical truth. With this in view, I choose to sing a different hymn than do the Galapagos Mountain Men or Hillsong United:

> Immortal, invisible, God only wise
> To all, life Thou givest, to both great and small
> And so let Thy glory, Almighty impart
> Through Christ in His story, Thy Christ to the heart.[116]

If God created man in his image and Christ gives life to us all, whether great or small, there is a premise for man's identity and parameters for his thinking and his behavior. Truth is objective, revealed in God's Word, and affirmed in the created order. However, if man is a material coincidence wandering in a multiverse governed by mindless chance, truth is meaningless. This leads us to the next progressive lie.

---

[115] David Berlinski. *The Devil's Delusion: Atheism and Its Scientific Pretensions* (Philadelphia, Pennsylvania: Perseus Books, 2009), 180.

[116] Walter C. Smith. "Immortal, Invisible, God Only Wise."

CHAPTER 3
RELATIVISM

"But what will become of men then?" I asked him, "without God and immortal life? All things are lawful then; they can do what they like."[117]
Dmitri Fyodorovitch in *The Brothers Karamazov*

And God said, "Let there be light."
Genesis 1:3

THE LIE IN THE CULTURE

Founded in 1868, the University of California set a course of higher education built upon the courage and resourcefulness of the people who populated the frontier state of California. "It is 'of the people and for the people,'" remarked its first president, Daniel Gilman, "not in any low or unworthy sense, but in the highest and noblest relations to their intellectual and moral well-being."[118] "Highest," "noblest," and "moral well-being" were not foreign to the first campus in Oakland, which had been initially conceived by Congregationalist minister Henry Durant before the University of California succeeded what had been the College of California. The University's corporate seal, approved in 1884, conveyed its aspirations: an open book crossed by a streamer carrying the University motto, Fiat Lux, or "Let There Be Light."

---

[117] Fyodor Dostoyevsky. *The Brothers Karamazov* (New York: Dover Publications, 2019), 715.

[118] "The University of California Is Born: How a World-Class University Got Its Start 150 Years Ago." https://tinyurl.com/4k88xvdh.

Together, the book and the streamer symbolized the discovery and spread of knowledge, in line with the University's founding purposes.[119]

Exactly a century later, in 1984, I would graduate from the University's San Diego campus, the beginning of a lifelong affiliation that continued through medical school, internal medicine residency, and faculty appointment. I am indebted to colleagues, physician trainees, and medical students who have inspired and challenged me over the ensuing years of my career. However, the ideas expressed in this book place me well outside of the cultural mainstream of the University of California, its values captured in a recent headline: "University president vows to protect abortion for 'pregnant people.'"[120] I am a member of a small and shrinking minority. I am left to wonder how the University that extols Fiat Lux (from Genesis 1:3) reached the point where a biblical Christian would feel like an ideological outsider? What happened to the "nobility" and "moral well-being" that were valued at the outset? In short, who turned out the lights?

The lies already introduced—materialism and evolutionism—provide the best explanation. They have been believed, and God has become irrelevant. And if there is no God, there is no certain truth to inform man's thinking nor moral standard to guide his behavior. Instead, man is alone, groping to find his way in the darkness. It is the outworking of this inescapable logic:

If God does not exist, then everything is permitted.
If materialism is true, then God does not exist.
If materialism is true, then everything is permitted.[121]

The Oxford English Dictionary defines relativism as "the doctrine that knowledge, truth, and morality exist in relation to culture, society, or historical context, and are not absolute."[122] The two words that

---

[119] The University of California Brand Guidelines. "The History of the Seal." https://tinyurl.com/566zw6ns.

[120] Jared Johnson. "University of California President Vows to Protect Abortion for 'Pregnant People.'" *The College Fix* (Jun. 2022). https://tinyurl.com/44zthe88.

[121] Berlinski, *The Devil's Delusion*, 19.

[122] Oxford Reference. "Relativism." https://tinyurl.com/4zuvj88a.

matter most in this definition are "not absolute." If there is no God, there can be no absolute knowledge, truth, or morality. Everything is relative, personal, and subjective. With his usual clarity, Berlinski explains: "If moral imperatives are not commanded by God's will, and if they are not in some sense absolute, then what ought to be is a matter simply of what men and women decide should be. There is no other source of judgment. What is this if not another way of saying that *if God does not exist, everything is permitted?*"[123]

After Darwin's publication of *On the Origin of Species* in 1859, it did not take long for the spiritual and moral consequences to manifest and for everyone to realize that, in a world in which God does not exist, everything is indeed permitted. German Philosopher Friedrich Nietzsche was among the first to fully grasp the near- and long-term portent of Darwinian evolution. Tom Wolfe summarizes Nietzsche's ominous vision:

> By 1874 Nietzsche had paid Darwin and his theory the highest praise with the most famous declaration in modern philosophy: "God is dead." Without mentioning Darwin by name, he said the "doctrine that there is no cardinal distinction between man and animal" will demoralize humanity throughout the West; it will lead to the rise of "barbaric nationalistic brotherhoods"—he all but called them by name: Nazism, Communism, and Fascism—and result within one generation in "wars such as never have been fought before." If we take one generation to be thirty years, that would have meant by 1904. In fact, the First World War broke out in 1914. This latter-day barbarism, he went on to say, will in the twenty-first century lead to something worse than the great wars: the total eclipse of all values.[124]

Among the first to fulfill this prophetic vision was Joseph Stalin. Born in 1878, he attended an ecclesiastical school and started out as a theist before turning to atheism under the trance of Darwinian

---

[123] Berlinski, *The Devil's Delusion*, 40.
[124] Wolfe, *The Kingdom of Speech*, 51.

evolution. G. Glurdjidze, one of Stalin's (Soso's) boyhood friends, recounts the decisive turn:

> I began to speak of God. Joseph heard me out, and after a moment's silence said: "You know, they are fooling us, there is no God ..." I was astonished at these words. I had never heard anything like it before. "How can you say such things, Soso?" I exclaimed. "I'll lend you a book to read; it will show you that the world and all living things are quite different from what you imagine, and all this talk about God is sheer nonsense," Joseph said. "What book is that?' I inquired. "Darwin. You must read it," Joseph impressed on me.[125]

One can only speculate what the course of the twentieth century might have been if Stalin had not read Darwin.

What we do know is how the twentieth century, an age in which scientific materialism reigned and faith in God declined, did in fact turn out. Between them, the three leading tyrants—two communists and one national socialist—slaughtered over eighty-seven million people: Mao claims forty million, Stalin twenty million, and Hitler seventeen million. This staggering toll excludes millions murdered by other communist regimes across Asia, Europe, Latin America, and Africa. In a world in which God does not exist, everything is permitted. "What Hitler did *not* believe and what Stalin did *not* believe and what Mao did *not* believe," adds Berlinski, "was that God was watching what they were doing."[126]

The new atheists have fought mightily to dissociate neo-Darwinian evolution from the likes of Hitler. Their problem is that Darwinian evolution enshrines its ethics in its methods of natural selection and survival of the fittest. Darwin betrays this in the full title of his signature book, *On the Origin of Species by Means of Natural Selection, or the Preservation of Favoured Races in the Struggle for Life*. Even

---

[125] Matt Leisola and Jonathan Witt. *Heretic: One Scientist's Journey from Darwin to Design* (Seattle, Washington: Discovery Institute, 2018), 132.

[126] Berlinski, *The Devil's Delusion*, 26.

Richard Dawkins reveals the true situation in the provocative title of his 1976 book, *The Selfish Gene*. Historian Richard Weikart puts the nail in the coffin in his carefully researched examination of the Darwinian worldview in relationship to the Nazis.

> Those wanting to distance Darwinism from the Nazis need to stop ignoring the fact that the racial inegalitarianism of the Nazis in the mid-twentieth century was not all that distant from the racist attitudes and theories of many Darwinian biologists, anthropologists, and physicians. Darwin himself was racist and exulted in the European extermination of the "lower races," which he integrated into his theory of human evolution. Many other scientists likewise promoted racism on the basis of their understanding of evolutionary theory. If the Nazi perspective was a misinterpretation of Darwinism, it was a misinterpretation fostered by the Darwinian biologists themselves, not by non-scientists or fringe publicists.[127]

Darwinian evolution not only eliminates God as a judge of right and wrong but replaces him with amoral determinism. Where human life is the outcome of impersonal, mindless, random processes playing out in an impersonal, mindless, random universe, who can really be held accountable for behavior? Free will, moral agency, and personal responsibility cease to exist. Thus, a psychology textbook can claim that genes predetermine decisions, an anthropologist that there is an evolutionary basis for rape, or a behavioral scientist that the social conduct of people has something to do with molecular pathways found in amoebae. John West, author of *Darwin Day in America*, argues that the age of science has become the age of materialism throughout American culture: "We are repeatedly told today that our behaviors, our emotions, even our moral and religious longings are reducible to some combination of physical processes interacting with our environment."[128]

---

[127] Richard Weikart. *Darwinian Racism: How Darwinism Influenced Hitler, Nazism, and White Nationalism* (Seattle, Washington: Discovery Institute, 2022), 11.

[128] John G. West. *Darwin Day in America: How Our Politics and Culture Have Been Dehumanized in the Name of Science* (Wilmington, Delaware: Intercollegiate Studies Institute,

With God removed from the equation, individuals are left to find their own way. This explains the emergence of the individual as the final judge of knowledge, truth, and morality. The primacy of the self speaks in expressions such as "my body, my choice," "I need to be authentic," "the real me," "my lived experience," or "my pronouns." Such phrases expose the unrealistic expectation that others conform to the demands of the self and affirm, as if true, every individual assertion and every individual reality, all the while vilifying anyone who is unsubmissive and therefore guilty of "othering." The demands of relativism are clear: there are as many truths, as many realities, as many moralities as there are people, or about eight billion. As Carl Trueman observes, "The modern self assumes the authority of feelings and sees authenticity as defined by the ability to give social expression to the same. The modern self also assumes that society at large will recognize and affirm this behavior."[129]

The modern self similarly assumes that God will recognize and affirm this behavior, making him, in the words of theologian Noelle Mering, "little more than an extension of ourselves or a therapeutic being who serves to comfort and affirm us. 'He must decrease, we must increase' is our modern mantra."[130]

What does this have to do with the University of California? The academy's worldview of materialism and evolutionism—its disbelief in God—leads it to view knowledge, truth, and morality in relativistic, subjective terms. This is the reason the President of the University of California can self-righteously vow to "protect abortion for 'pregnant people,'" simultaneously endorsing the greatest holocaust of the modern era and abolishing the most basic biological distinction between men and women. This is the spiritual darkness of the University of California. It is immoral and anti-scientific. Everything is permitted, and nothing is absolute.

2007), Loc 105, Kindle.

[129] Carl R. Trueman. *Strange New World: How Thinkers and Activists Redefined Identity and Sparked the Sexual Revolution* (Wheaton, Illinois: Crossway, 2022), 19.

[130] Noelle Mering. *Awake, Not Woke: A Christian Response to the Cult of Progressive Ideology* (Gastonia, North Carolina: TAN Books, 2021), 27.

The same darkness has spread across the broader culture. Having already embraced scientific materialism, American institutions, from education and entertainment to business and government, have embraced relativism regarding truth and morality. It is the reason for the wide acceptance of the progressive lies of abortion, homosexuality, transgenderism, and neo-Marxist critical theory. In the 2020 American Worldview Inventory, when asked where Americans find "truth," a sizeable majority (58 percent) of respondents rejected the idea of absolute truth, citing instead sources such as "inner certainty," "scientific proof," "tradition," or "public consensus"; the minority held that "God is the basis of truth."[131] This corresponds to a growing pessimism about the moral climate of the country. In a 2022 Gallup survey, when asked to rate the overall state of moral values in the United States today, a record 50 percent described it as "poor," the lowest possible rating.[132]

THE LIE IN THE CHURCH

With evolutionism controlling the historical denominations and spreading into American evangelicalism, it is no surprise that the thread of relativism weaves not only through the culture but also deep into the church. In its concessions to scientific materialism, the progressive church has surrendered its hold on biblical truth and biblical morality. By embracing evolutionism, it has embraced its moral corollary, relativism. Rather than being light in the darkness, the progressive church has become itself a place of darkness. There is no greater darkness than of a church that has lost its way. It is perhaps this kind of self-deception that Jesus had in mind when he said, "If then the light in you is darkness, how great is the darkness!"[133]

Forty years ago, Francis Schaeffer, a prophetic voice in his time, would worry that the church is naïve to the real struggle in which it was engaged—a struggle of worldviews.

---

[131] George Barna. "Americans See Many Sources of Truth—And Reject Moral Absolutes." https://tinyurl.com/4v2s5udp.
[132] "Moral Issues." *Gallup News.* https://tinyurl.com/bdtvubnh.
[133] Matthew 6:23.

The basic problem of the Christians in this country in the last eighty years or so, in regard to society and in regard to government, is that they have ... failed to see that all of this has come about due to a shift in worldview—that is, through a fundamental change in the overall way people think and view the world and life as a whole. This shift has been *away from* a worldview that was at least vaguely Christian in people's memory (even if they were not individually Christian) *toward* something completely different—toward a worldview based upon the idea that the final reality is impersonal matter or energy shaped into its present form by impersonal choice.[134]

Many in the church still fail to see that the culture war is, at its root, between two competing worldviews—one biblical, one materialistic. Others have surrendered the fight and joined the other side.

"Science in general and evolution in particular," notes Peter Enns, "made knowledge-based Christians in the nineteenth century with Bibles in hand very nervous, and for good reason. And things haven't gotten much better."[135] For Enns, this is reflected in a loss of "certainty" and "adjusting our expectations about what the Bible can deliver."[136] The uncertainty that follows turns not to Scripture for resolution but inward: "Rather than defining faithfulness as absolute conformity to authority ... a trust-centered faith will value in others the search for true human authenticity that may take them away from the familiar borders of their faith, while trusting God to be part of that process in ourselves and others, even those closest to us."[137] Absolutes recede in favor of human authenticity, blurring the borders of knowledge, truth, and morality.

Then Vineyard USA pastor Ken Wilson takes a somewhat different tack in his *Letter to My Congregation*, with this lengthy but revealing

---

[134] Francis A. Schaeffer. *A Christian Manifesto* (Wheaton, Illinois: Crossway, 1981), 17-18.
[135] Enns, *The Sin of Certainty*, 36.
[136] Enns, *The Sin of Certainty*, 152.
[137] Enns, *The Sin of Certainty*, 210.

subtitle: *An evangelical pastor's path to embracing people who are gay, lesbian, bisexual, and transgender into the company of Jesus.* As progressives are wont to do, he diminishes the authority of Scripture on the one hand while reinterpreting it on the other. Thus, he affirms evolution and diminishes the biblical account of Genesis as "creation stories." At the same time, he reinterprets inconvenient passages prohibitive of sexual intimacy outside of monogamous, heterosexual marriage. It is a "have-your-cake-and-eat-it-too" approach to biblical interpretation and doctrine. It is relativistic, selective, and subjective, for it empowers the interpreter to apply a personal lens to any text to clarify its meaning and achieve the desired outcome. Everything is up for grabs. Everything is permissible.

Arguably the most significant proponent of this approach in the past century was Joseph Fletcher. An Episcopalian priest, he applied himself to thinking about the relationship of Scripture to ethics. Situation ethics, as he terms it, was transformative both within and outside of the church, responsible, to a large degree, for the social realities observed today in bioethics and sexual ethics. Situation ethics is a variation of relativism applied to a broad range of social circumstances. Fletcher summarizes his premise: "I think there are no normative moral principles whatsoever which are intrinsically valid or universally obliging … Whether we ought to follow a moral principle or not would, I contend, always depend upon the situation." He offers these six guiding propositions:

1. Only one thing is intrinsically good, namely love: nothing else.
2. The ultimate norm of Christian decisions is love: nothing else.
3. Love and justice are the same, for justice is love distributed.
4. Love wills the neighbor's good whether we like him or not.
5. Only the end justifies the means: nothing else.
6. Decisions ought to be made situationally, not prescriptively.[138]

---

[138] Joseph Fletcher and John Warwick Montgomery. *Situation Ethics—True or False: A Dialogue Between Joseph Fletcher and John Warwick Montgomery* (Irvine, California: New Reformation, 1972), 16.

One can hear the echo of Fletcher's ethic in the "love is love" tautology often repeated to justify sexual perversion. Indeed, on a situational basis, and with his distorted version of "love" in mind, Fletcher justifies abortion, thievery, dishonesty, and fornication. This arbitrary and man-centered ethic is itself absolutist, entirely dismissive of the moral standards of Scripture. Fletcher would eventually dispense with the Bible and pursue his own path as an atheist.

How widespread is relativistic thinking among Christians? The 2020 American Worldview Inventory asked this of evangelical Christians, defined as "those believing the Bible to be the true, reliable word of God." The survey found evangelicals are no more likely to accept absolute moral truth (48 percent) than they are to reject it (46 percent). Among "born-again Christians," a mere 43 percent still embrace the notion of absolute truth. However, those who specifically embrace a "biblical worldview" are more than twice as likely to see God as the basis of truth (96 percent versus 38 percent) and to reject the idea that moral absolutes do not exist (85 percent).[139] These data support the premise that worldview matters immensely and distinguishes between evangelicals who accept or reject relativism. They indicate that a significant proportion of self-identified evangelicals mirror the larger culture in rejecting God as a basis of truth and rejecting moral absolutes.

Relativism thrives inside the progressive church precisely because the biblical premise for moral absolutes—a God who created the universe and man in his image—has been removed. Unless and until this is restored, knowledge, truth, and morality will continue to be free-floating. The basic defect of the progressive church, grounded in its scientistic acceptance of materialism and evolutionism, is that it stands in judgment of Scripture, not Scripture of it. Scientism takes the place of biblicism, and human, relativistic judgments replace God's eternal, absolute truth. Upcoming chapters will discuss the downstream implications of this disastrous worldview: abortionism, omnisexualism, transgenderism, and communism.

---

[139] Barna, "Americans See Many Sources of Truth."

If the materialist worldview is correct in its relativism or if biblical principles can be selectively applied based on situational factors, then everything is permissible. There are no absolutes, and there is no truth. Biblical Christians are deluded and judgmental. It is time to wave the white flag and surrender to the opinion leaders in the culture. But they are lying.

THE BIBLICAL TRUTH

After the creation of the heavens and the earth, Moses' account continues: "And God said, 'Let there be light,' and there was light. And God saw that the light was good. And God separated the light from the darkness."[140] This passage speaks of the creation of energy, of light waves and particles. This text also highlights a more profound point of the creation narrative. When God said, "Let there be light," he created something that was "good" beyond the excellence of physical light. He created something "good" in the spiritual, holy, and godly sense. This light does not radiate from hot suns across the galaxies but from the blazing, pure, and noble character of God.

This understanding of Genesis is underscored by John's parallel account. Not only is Jesus "the Word" who was with God in the beginning and through whom all things were made. Jesus is also the light: "In him was life, and the life was the light of men. The light shines in the darkness, and the darkness has not overcome it."[141] Jesus is not only the Creator of all life, but he is also the source of all light. This makes sense from nature, in which sunlight is the essential source of life-giving energy for our planet. The same is true spiritually: Jesus is the light that makes spiritual life possible.

Jesus astounded his disciples and angered his detractors when he said, "I am the light of the world. Whoever follows me will not walk in darkness but will have the light of life."[142] Jesus confirms not only his divinity as Creator but also his embodiment of all truth and all

---

[140] Genesis 1:3-4.
[141] John 1:4-5.
[142] John 8:12.

righteousness. He is the source of all that is good and moral. He is the judge of what is right and wrong, just and unjust, true and false. He is the light that exposes the darkness, all that is evil, perverted, sinful, and unholy. This light is eternal, just as God's Word is timeless, unchanging, and absolute. It was, and is, and always will be. There is no recess of the galaxies nor recess of the human mind that is beyond its exposure.

Spiritual reality comes down to light and dark. It is straightforward. It is two-sided. There are no gray scales, no half-truths, no muddied waters. God's Word confronts man with stark choices between the true and the false, between the right and the wrong, between obedience and disobedience, between life and death. Nothing is relative. Everything is absolute.

The prophets expressed their moral concerns with dichotomous clarity, calling people to repent of sin and turn to righteousness. But they also warned against deceivers who would attempt to play the modernist card of moral relativism to confuse matters. Isaiah thus warns:

Woe to those who call evil good and good evil,
Who put darkness for light and light for darkness,
Who put bitter for sweet and sweet for bitter![143]

Like the prophets, Jesus presents his hearers with straightforward choices. They may take the wide path or the narrow path, enter the wide gate or the narrow gate, enjoy the world for a season or invest in heaven for eternity, build upon the rock or build upon the sand. This is why faith comes more naturally to children, or child-like adults; these are the ones for whom moral decision-making is easiest and least complicated.

The epistles of John elaborate this biblical worldview, echoing themes in John's Gospel. As graphically represented below, John's first epistle delineates two realms. The first is the realm of light and truth with God as its Father and ruler: "God is light, and in him is no darkness at all."[144] His children include all who have been reborn in

---

[143] Isaiah 5:20.

Christ and thus belong to the family of God, or the church. The children of God are distinguished by their love for God ("for love is from God, and whoever loves has been born of God and knows God"[145]), their love for one another ("Whoever loves his brother abides in the light"[146]), and their obedience to God's commands ("And by this we know that we have come to know him, if we keep his commandments"[147]). The second is the realm of darkness and lies with Satan as its father and ruler. His children include all who have been naturally born, who have joined Satan in his sinful rebellion: "Whoever makes a practice of sinning is of the devil, for the devil has been sinning from the beginning."[148] Such children are against (anti) Christ. These children are distinguished by their love of the world and their hatred of God: "If anyone loves the world, the love of the Father is not in him."[149] Their disobedience of God's commands ("By this it is evident ... who are the children of the devil: whoever does not practice righteousness is not of God"[150]) and hate for one another ("But whoever hates his brother is in the darkness and walks in the darkness"[151]) confirm their allegiance to the darkness. There is no middle ground between these two realms. "If we say we have fellowship with him while we walk in darkness, we lie and do not practice the truth."[152] In this biblical reality, it is impossible at the same time to love God and love the world, to love God and hate one another, or to love God and disobey him. It is one way or the other. It is all or none.

---

[144] 1 John 1:5.
[145] 1 John 4:7.
[146] 1 John 2:10.
[147] 1 John 2:3.
[148] 1 John 3:8.
[149] 1 John 2:15.
[150] 1 John 3:10.
[151] 1 John 2:11.
[152] 1 John 1:6.

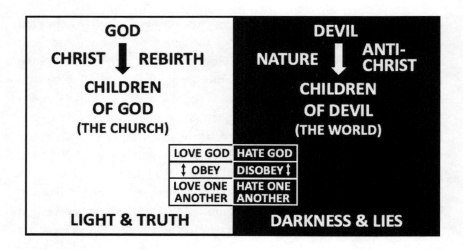

A point upon which John is clear, and very unmodern, is that love cannot exist without truth. In his second epistle, John's opening salutation goes this way: "The elder to the elect lady and her children, whom I *love in truth*."[153] The opening to his third epistle is very similar: "The elder to the beloved Gaius, whom I *love in truth*."[154] John expresses his abiding affection in terms of truth: "For I rejoiced greatly when the brothers came and testified to your truth, as indeed you are walking in the truth. I have no greater joy than to hear that my children are walking in the truth."[155] John is saying that love and truth are more than complementary. They are inextricably connected. It is therefore impossible to love outside of truth. The inclusive "love is love" expression finds no scriptural support.

The relativistic worldview promoted by materialism and evolutionism puts truth up for grabs and turns moral standards upside down. In sharp contrast, the biblical perspective embraces truth and establishes moral order and clarity. Three take-home lessons emerge in terms of spiritual strategy, spiritual tactics, and spiritual priorities.

Strategically, Christians in the authentic church must come to grips with the reality of the current situation: warfare. Two worldviews—one

---

[153] 2 John 1.
[154] 3 John 1.
[155] 3 John 3-4.

biblical and spiritual, one material and secular—are in mortal conflict. Neither can compromise. No armistice can be negotiated. No peace can be concluded. It is a struggle to the death. Francis Schaeffer grasped this forty years ago, when the battle was not nearly as intense as it is today. But he would have affirmed that the progressive lies being recounted in this book originate from a false worldview originating from an ungodly place of darkness and deception. They originate in the mind of Satan, who, since the Garden of Eden, has been at war with God and his people.

A veteran missionary friend would often reflect upon his journey with this metaphor: "Life is a battlefield, not a playground." He understood what it meant to be a Christian in a hostile world, and he understood the sacrifices that were required to be victorious. The church will not win the battle before her if she does not comprehend the spiritual struggle that it is. If she is unserious, as if on a playground, she will only invite casualties and defeat. She must decide whether she will enjoin the battle in obedience to God or flee the conflict in hopes of an elusive peace. As Presbyterian scholar J. Gresham Machen realized in his own valiant struggle against liberalism and modernism in the early twentieth century, "In the sphere of religion, as in other spheres, the things about which men are agreed are apt to be the things that are least worth holding; the really important things are the things about which men will fight."[156]

Tactically, this battle must be waged with truth. Truth is the weapon that demolishes false arguments and destroys the enemy's strongholds. Truth is a sword—"the sword of the Spirit, which is the word of God"[157]—that conquers lies and vacates deceptions. The truth of God's Word is eternal and universal. It transcends culture and politics. It is absolute and unchanging. There is no such thing as "relative" truth. If it is "relative," if it is changed by cultural circumstances, if it is subject to personal reinterpretation, it is not truth.

This calls for a return of individuals, families, and churches to the Bible as the only book of importance, as the rule for what we know,

---

[156] Machen, *Christianity and Liberalism*, Loc 93.
[157] Ephesians 6:17.

how we think, and the way we live. It should preoccupy our thoughts, fill our memories, illuminate our insights, correct our attitudes, and frame our decisions. Any compromise of Scripture, any discounting of its authority, or any deviation from its commands is a concession to the adversary. Relativistic preaching, relativistic thinking, and relativistic living can only lead to destruction. Anything at variance with God's Word must be rejected. Anything in accord with his Word—both its compelling love and uncompromising truth—is embraced.

There is a large segment of the Christian community that is embarrassed by God's Word. Rather than communicate God's Word clearly to the culture or even to the church, its sharp edges are smoothed, and its convicting message is softened. Too many believe that the culture can be won with clever, compromising strategies. Instead of the authority of Scripture, they pursue a more pragmatic, winsome approach in vain expectation of success. To the extent that this has been the church's de facto strategy, in lieu of aggressive spiritual combat, it has come up decidedly short. The church has lost its power, its authority, and its conviction. Instead of being an influence upon the culture, it has acquiesced to it. Instead of being "the light of the world," the church has put the lamp of truth under a basket.[158] "The weakness of most Christians today," concludes Mering, "is not that we are too strident but that we are too cowardly."[159]

Why does it matter? It comes down to priorities. There is only one thing that ultimately matters—the eternal destiny of each living soul. The only thing that matters is whether eternity is spent with God in heaven or apart from him in hell. It is the only thing that matters for each member of one's family, church, and neighborhood. What does *not* matter is how much money is made, how much success is achieved, or how much renown is attained. Jesus put it concisely: "For what does it profit a man to gain the whole world and forfeit his soul?"[160] The answer to this rhetorical question hangs on each listener's lips: "Nothing!"

---

[158] Matthew 5:14-15.
[159] Mering, *Awake Not Woke*, 17.
[160] Mark 8:36.

If the spoils of the war of worldviews are nothing less than eternal souls, it should make a difference in how life is ordered. This is the reason I am writing this book. It starts with a priority concern for my family, my children. I know that their eternal destinies rest upon a relationship with Christ grounded in his Word. It requires that they think biblically in response to the lies that are being told to them. If they are not equipped, their spiritual future is in doubt. The question begging a response from every believer is this: will I engage in this fight on behalf of those I love, or will I shrink from the battle in cowardly fear?

CHAPTER 4
ABORTIONISM

To have an abortion out of loving concern for everybody's best interests involved is not an excusably evil thing to do, but a good thing to do.[161]
Joseph Fletcher

So God created man in his own image, in the image of God he created him.
Genesis 1:27

THE LIE IN THE CULTURE

There is no more horrific indicator of the toll of the materialist, evolutionist worldview upon American society than the nearly sixty-five million preborn children murdered since the dreadful Supreme Court decision in *Roe* a half century ago. This worldview reduces preborn children to the sum of their randomly assembled, material components, stripping them of their intrinsic value. It robs preborn children of their most basic, God-given right, the right to life, without which all other rights cease to exist. In 1976, a mere three years after *Roe*, Francis Schaeffer would squarely assign responsibility for abortion where it most belongs, upon the worldview exemplified by materialist Francis Crick, co-discoverer of the DNA double helix.

---

[161] Fletcher, *Situation Ethics—True or False*, 31.

If man is what Francis Crick says he is, then he is only the sum of the impersonal *plus* time *plus* chance; he is nothing more than the energy particle extended and more complex. Our own generation can thus disregard human life. On the one end we kill the embryo through abortion—and on the other end we will introduce euthanasia for the old. The one is already here, and the door is opened for the other.[162]

The connections between Darwinian evolution and abortion lie close to the surface. Darwin himself would identify it as a means of population control, potentially more potent than the "checks" of famine or natural disasters: "Malthus has discussed these several checks, but he does not lay stress enough on what is probably the most important of all, namely, infanticide, especially of female infants, and the habit of procuring abortion … as a means of keeping down the population."[163] Darwin's matter-of-fact descriptions of female infanticide and human abortion are chilling.

Social Darwinism quickly spread across Europe and the United States. Natural selection was a convenient theory for designating certain categories of people, particularly certain races, as unfit and for justifying population controls. Darwinism thus provided intellectual support not only for racism but also for racial extermination, including the use of abortion and euthanasia.[164] The Nazis perfected this in their efforts to purge the German race of undesirables, including not only Jews but also Germans with disabilities and chronic diseases.[165] They controlled reproduction through forced sterilization and abortion, justified by a conditional value of life ethic under which some lives are deemed not worth living.

The Communists were not to be out done. Dedicated materialists that they were, they too enthusiastically accepted abortion as another way to devalue what to them was nothing more than human capital.

---

[162] Francis A. Schaeffer. *How Should We Then Live* (Wheaton, Illinois: Crossway, 1976), 234.
[163] Darwin, *The Descent of Man*, Loc 892.
[164] Weikart, *Darwinian Racism*, 11.
[165] Leo Alexander. "Medical Science under Dictatorship." *New England Journal of Medicine* 241 (1949), 44.

Whittaker Chambers describes his personal experience as an underground American communist in the 1920s and the 1930s, decades before *Roe* was decided.

> As an underground Communist, I took it for granted that children were out of the question. Not only left-wing and underground Communists took such matters for granted. Abortion was a commonplace of party life. There were Communist doctors who rendered that service for a small fee. Communists who were more choosy knew liberal doctors who would render the same service for a larger free. Abortion, which now fills me with physical horror, I then regarded, like all Communists, as a mere physical manipulation.[166]

The eugenics of social Darwinism realized its fullest expression in the United States in the work of Margaret Sanger, the infamous founder of Planned Parenthood. She advocated abortion ("the most merciful thing that the large family does to one of its infant members is to kill it"), eugenics ("the gradual suppression, elimination, and eventual extinction of defective stocks—those human weeds which threaten the blooming of the finest flowers of American civilization"), and racism ("feeblemindedness perpetuates itself from the ranks of those who are blandly indifferent to their racial responsibilities").[167] Her evil ideology has caused no small amount of historical revisionism among Planned Parenthood supporters. But the legacy continues in the disproportionate presence of Planned Parenthood in minority neighborhoods and the disproportionate number of minority babies—especially black babies—who have been murdered, making all the stranger the enduring alliance of black liberals and the abortion movement (the 1966 recipient of Planned Parenthood's Margaret Sanger Award was none other than Martin Luther King).[168] Sanger's grandson, chair of the International Planned Parenthood Council, is unwavering in his Darwinian apology

---

[166] Chambers, *Witness*, 273.
[167] State of Arizona Senate, SCR 1026. https://tinyurl.com/56wyef87.
[168] Planned Parenthood Federation of America Margaret Sanger Award Winners; Recipients 1966–2015. https://tinyurl.com/2s37mvj6.

for the holocaust that his grandmother helped bring about, his words laced with Orwellian double-speak.

> Humanity has evolved to take conscious control of reproduction and has done so in order to survive and preserve life. Taking control of reproduction is respectful of life. At times it means not conceiving a life, and sometimes it means not letting unborn life be born. When humanity does this, it often does so in pursuance of a reproductive strategy that will best enable it to preserve and nurture other life. We cannot repeal the laws of natural selection. Nature does not let every life form survive. Humanity uniquely, and to its benefit, can exercise some dominion over this process and maximize the chance for human life to survive and grow.[169]

In the United States, the justification of abortion is sanitized of its Darwinian origins. The heinous deed must be given a more soothing demeanor. It is therefore framed as "reproductive health," "privacy rights," or "bodily autonomy." This is attached to moral justifications that conceal the dark motivations that otherwise explain the wanton murder of a preborn child. Joseph Fletcher provides a situational defense of abortion and, with a sleight of hand, converts it from a wrong to a positive good.

> It is ethically foolish to say we "ought" to do what is wrong! What I want to argue philosophically, with respect to the issue over the locus of value in human acts, is that the rightness or the wrongness of anything we do is extrinsic, relative, and dependent upon the circumstances, so that to have an abortion out of loving concern for everybody's best interest involved, is not an excusably evil thing to do, but a good thing to do.[170]

---

[169] Alexander Sanger. *Beyond Choice: Reproductive Freedom and the 21st Century* (New York: Public Affairs, 2004), 292.

[170] Fletcher, *Situation Ethics—True or False*, 31.

In the end, any justification of abortion must place the narrowly defined self-interest of the mother above all. This discounts the interest of the preborn child in determining the aggregate best interest. In fact, the interests of the preborn are excluded from the calculus altogether. Would any preborn child opt for painful dismemberment? This is where the hyper-focus on self, so characteristic of the modern, materialist mindset, is shown for what it is: the loathing of another. Trueman describes how this math might be used by a couple inspired by expressive individualism to decide the fate of a preborn child with a birth defect: "Abortion or even euthanasia after birth can be justified because the net amount of happiness for the persons involved (only the adults, not the newborn) will be greater if the child is killed."[171]

Sadly, abortion attitudes in the United States betray the relativism expected of a culture that embraces Darwinian evolution. In early 2022, before the conclusion of the *Dobbs* case reversing *Roe*, the Pew Research Center conducted a survey of U.S. adults. What do Americans have to say? Most believe that abortion should be legal.[172] Only 37 percent believe abortion should be illegal with exceptions; a miniscule 8 percent say that abortion should be illegal in all circumstances. One in three adults simultaneously hold that life begins at conception and that the abortion decision should be left to the woman!

More disturbing are the actual abortion statistics to which these attitudes correspond. The most reliable totals come from the Guttmacher Institute, who reports 930,160 abortions in 2020, the most recent year for which data are available.[173] This is a decline from a peak in 1990, though this trend may exclude some of the growing number of medication ("self-managed") abortions or unreported surgical abortions. There were 14.4 abortions per 1000 women aged 15 to 44, a stunning rate that climbs even higher to 23.8 abortions per 1,000 non-Hispanic Black women, this in keeping with the racist history of abortion in America. Guttmacher's preliminary data also finds that 2020 was "the first time that more than half of all abortions in clinical settings in the

---

[171] Trueman, *Strange New World*, 157.
[172] Pew Research Center. "America's Abortion Quandary." https://tinyurl.com/2pkbckhm.
[173] Jeff Diamant and Besheer Mohamde. "What the Data Says About Abortion in the U.S." *Pew Research Center* (2022). https://tinyurl.com/2p98zdmt.

U.S. were medication abortions."[174] Abortion remains far and away the leading cause of death in the United States, trailed by heart disease (696,962) and cancer (602,350).[175] Uncounted are the many children conceived by in vitro fertilization (IVF), 93 percent of whom never reach term, as "most either dwell eternally frozen in the lab, are deemed 'non-viable' by the gods of science and thawed for discard, won't survive the transfer from freezer to womb, or are ~~aborted~~ 'selectively reduced' if too many embryos implant."[176]

Behind these unconscionable statistics are precious individuals known only to God, each ruthlessly murdered by a culture that has turned not only on God but upon itself.

THE LIE IN THE CHURCH

Just as the lies of materialism, evolutionism, and relativism have justified abortion in the culture, so they have justified abortion in the minds of many in the American church. Progressives in the church have propagated the misnomers of "reproductive health," "privacy rights," and "bodily autonomy." They have promoted the logic of *Roe* in denying the right to life to the preborn. They have advanced Fletcher's situation ethics to recast murder as a positive good. They have voted pro-abortion candidates into political office while voting anti-abortion candidates out. They have rejected a biblical worldview, rejected the authority of God's Word, and rejected truth. They have welcomed the darkness into the church.

The mainline, historic Christian traditions in the United States have completely capitulated to abortionism, just as they have to evolutionism. Bemoaning the possible end of "safe and legal abortion" in the United States, the official Presbyterian Church (USA)'s website advances abortion as "reproductive justice." "Currently, the PC

---

[174] Rachel K. Jones et al. Guttmacher Institute. "Medication Abortion Now Accounts for More Than Half of All Abortions." *Guttmacher Institute* (2022). https://tinyurl.com/4beazhr4.

[175] National Center for Health Statistics, Centers for Disease Control and Prevention. https://tinyurl.com/yc5fkyr9.

[176] Katy Faust and Stacy Manning. "Shocking New York Times Article Illuminates that in Vitro Fertilization Means Babies Built to Order." *The Federalist* (Jun. 22, 2021). https://tinyurl.com/yfjv4csn.

(USA)'s office of Mission Responsibility Through Investment supports reproductive justice through shareholder activism, and the church's Social Justice and Peacemaking Unit works with the interdenominational Religious Coalition for Reproductive Choice."[177] This mouthful of political correctness is a defense of the *Roe* status quo. "It (*Roe v. Wade*) provided a legal framework to guide those trying to make responsible decisions regarding the possible termination of a pregnancy and it affirmed in the strongest terms the constitutional right of a pregnant woman to decide procedures and outcomes that involved her own body."[178] As "a church that has wrestled with this issue for decades," the progressive Presbyterian Church has tapped out in submission to the culture and against the preborn.

The Evangelical Lutheran Church in America has also fallen in line with the culture, though in a more nuanced way. Surrendering the hope of any absolute standard, they acknowledge that differences over the matter of abortion "are also a gift that can lead us into constructive conversation about our faith and its implications for our life in the world."[179] Their approach is a variation of the "safe, legal, and rare" position first fabricated by Bill Clinton. "Abortion ought to be an option only of last resort. Therefore, as a church we seek to reduce the need to turn to abortion as the answer to unintended pregnancies." In the end, the interests of women override the interests of the preborn. "Regardless of the decisions, our pastoral response must be a gracious affirmation of the value of women's lives and assistance in dealing with ongoing implications of their decisions for their own well-being and their relationships."

The United Methodist Church (UMC) position is arguably the most deceiving. While affirming "the sanctity of unborn human life," the UMC further understands "that the pregnant woman is also a life of sacred worth, and that there are circumstances in which there may be

---

[177] Nick Skaggs and David Staniunas. "Reproductive Justice and the PC(USA): General Assemblies, Church Advocacy and Abortion." *Presbyterian Historical Society* (2022). https://tinyurl.com/4962ad6h.

[178] J. Herbert Nelson. "As Abortion Debate Grows, State Clerk Reminds Church of General Assembly Policy." *Office of the General Assembly* (May, 2019). https://tinyurl.com/2p8sy7ca.

[179] Evangelical Lutheran Church in America. "Abortion." https://tinyurl.com/2u3vku9a.

'tragic conflicts of life versus life.' This may happen to any pregnant woman, anywhere, at any time during her pregnancy." The darkness closes in as the UMC argument descends into the devilish details of situation ethics.

> Critical to preserving life is ready access to proper medical care. This includes access to medical care that may include abortion when that is the way to preserve the most life possible. That is why the Social Principles affirm that in such cases we support the legal option of abortion under proper medical procedures by certified medical providers.[180]

While the progressive Presbyterian, Lutheran, and Methodist arguments draw inspiration more from the culture than Scripture, others simply reinterpret the Bible to fit the need. This is how Peter Enns finds space around the sixth commandment ("thou shalt not kill") to accommodate abortion. He does so with a nod to situation ethics.

> In other words, there seems to be a *situational* dimension to law … Law is God's revelation, but does that necessarily imply that it is static and unbending? Perhaps God himself understands—and in fact shows us—that even the law has a situational dimension … Few Christians would have any argument against the sixth commandment but believing it in principle is very different from acting upon it. Is capital punishment murder? What about abortion? What about protecting your family against an intruder? What about war? When we put flesh on the bare bones of the Ten Commandments, we see that there is a "wisdom dimension" to any attempt to keep the law.[181]

Theologian and former pastor Brian McLaren proposes "a new kind of Christianity" in a book by the same title. Leader of the "emerging

---

[180] The United Methodist Church. "What is the UM Position on Abortion?" https://tinyurl.com/2s3u6c77.

[181] Enns, *Inspiration and Incarnation*, 77.

church," which is Protestant and evangelical in its roots, he revisits Darwin when calling into question both the authority of Scripture and the biblical prohibition of abortion. He specifically challenges the Bible as "a divinely dictated science textbook."

> This approach has set up Christians on the wrong side of truth again and again—from Galileo's time, to Darwin's, to our own ... We are in trouble in relation to ethics. The Bible, when taken as an ethical rule book, offers us no clear categories for many of our most significant and vexing socio-ethical quandaries. We find no explicit mention, for example, of abortion ...[182]

McLaren sees the Bible as irrelevant to the ethical issues of the day since the precise language is absent, in this case, the word "abortion." McLaren is certainly theologian enough to be able to connect biblical ethics to the determination of whether a woman can murder her preborn child. This is a dodge.

Though not a bioethicist, Francis Collins has been at the forefront of hot button ethical issues as Director of the National Institutes of Health (NIH). His commitment to evolutionism appears to have cancelled his evangelical faith. Under his leadership, the NIH has funded research using the body parts of aborted human fetuses and created a "Tissue Hub" for collecting human fetal tissue samples ranging in age from six to forty-two weeks gestation. He has declined to condemn the abortion of infants with Down's Syndrome, stating, "In our current society, people are in a circumstance of being able to take advantage of those technologies (i.e., abortions). And we have decided as a society that that choice needs to be defended."[183] His translation of the human genome as "the language of God" has somehow not helped him figure out when life begins.

---

[182] Brian D. McLaren. *A New King of Christianity: Ten Questions That Are Transforming the Faith* (Sydney: Harper Collins, 2010), 68.

[183] John G. West. "NIH Director Francis Collins Isn't a National Treasure, He's a National Disgrace." *The Federalist* (Oct. 8, 2021), https://tinyurl.com/s9vprcb8.

Scientists, philosophers, and theologians have debated for centuries the point at which life actually begins. Deriving more information about the actual anatomical and molecular steps involved in the early development of the human embryo has not really helped with those debates, as this is not really a scientific question ... There is therefore (from a biologist's perspective) no convenient biological dividing line between a human being and an embryonic form that might be called "not quite there yet."[184]

Beguiled by influential progressive voices inside of the church, the pro-abortion leanings of many evangelicals are predictable. Fully one in three self-described evangelical Christians believes that abortion should be legal in all or most circumstances, according to a 2014 Pew Research Center study. Among those who hold to an evolutionary (naturalistic) worldview, the number rises to 55 percent.[185] More recent research has detected an uptick in younger evangelicals who are pro-abortion, increasing from 34 percent to 38 percent between 2016 and 2020.[186]

Behind these statistics are abortion-supporting individuals who sit next to us at church, attend the youth group, lead in worship, teach a Bible study, or even serve as pastors, deacons, and elders. They are not few, and they are among us. Yuh-Line Niou is an exemplary progressive Christian. A thirty-eight-year-old candidate for New York State Assembly for the 65th district, Niou boasted of her good standing at Tim Keller's Redeemer Presbyterian Church while also earning a perfect score from Planned Parenthood for her abortion views.[187]

Then again, perhaps Niou is right. Maybe abortion is a complex, situational matter that should be decided between a woman and her physician. Perhaps Enns and McLaren are correct that the Bible is of little use in making an abortion decision. And who is to say that

---

[184] Collins, *The Language of God*, 249.

[185] "Religious Landscape Study: Views About Abortion Among Evangelical Protestants." *Pew Research Center*. https://tinyurl.com/2fsy4r4f.

[186] Ryan P. Burge. "What's New in Evangelical Views on Abortion? The Age Gap." *Christianity Today* (Jan. 21, 2022). https://tinyurl.com/mrxdn9wc.

[187] "Tim Keller Is Pastor to Politician with Perfect Score from Planned Parenthood." *Capstone Report* (Jun. 12, 2022). https://tinyurl.com/ypp9urvv.

life begins at conception when Francis Collins does not know for sure? But they are lying.

THE BIBLICAL TRUTH

The first chapter of Genesis tells us that man is made in God's image, stating the fact not once, not twice, but three times. This repetition is neither accidental nor confusion on God's part. Instead, it is God's emphatic way of making his point clear. Man *is* in the image of God. This means that each person has measureless worth because each life is etched with God's likeness. The value of each person is not qualified by age, sex, race, health, or socio-economic status. It is intrinsic, constant, and essential. This unconditional value is not assigned at the point of viability, the moment of birth, graduation from kindergarten, or completion of college. It is assigned the moment that life begins, at conception.

The mark of God's image establishes God's sovereignty over every human life. Thus, God prohibits murder and suicide: "Whoever sheds the blood of man, by man shall his blood be shed, for God made man in his image."[188] This verse not only prohibits murder but requires justice for those who commit murder. With sixty-five million image-bearers murdered in America over the last half century, the thought of this reckoning is fearsome. While God is love, he is also just.

That life begins at conception is confirmed by the Incarnation. When the Word became flesh, the Son of God was conceived in the womb of a virgin, in the womb of Mary. Jesus started as a divinely fertilized egg. The Incarnation required that he repeat the same journey of life that all people complete, a journey that began as a single cell in the womb of his mother. The Incarnation commenced the instant Jesus was conceived. Jesus was not the incarnate Son of God after the first or second trimester. He was not the incarnate Son of God at the time of quickening. Nor was he the incarnate Son of God when he passed some arbitrary line of viability. And he was not the incarnate Son of God after he was born. No, he was the Son of God when he was conceived. That

---

[188] Genesis 9:6.

is the moment at which his identification with mankind began, his redemptive mission started, and a long journey got under way that would take him to the Cross where he died on our behalf.

Given that life begins at conception, any human intervention to arrest the development of the preborn child is murder. Abortion in any form is murder. Surgical abortion is murder. Medication abortion is murder. The use of abortifacient drugs is murder. The selective destruction or discarding of human embryos conceived through in vitro fertilization is murder. The killing of a mother carrying a preborn baby is twice murder.

The "whoever" in Genesis 9:6 is anyone who participates in the bloodshed. This would include any medical professional who advises, assists in, or performs an abortion, whether through surgical or medical means. It includes friends or family who counsel in favor of an abortion, pay for an abortion, or drive someone to an abortion. It includes pastors and spiritual leaders who have taught in favor of abortion or failed to speak against it. It includes the mother and father who schedule the appointment, attend the appointment, and willingly consent to the abortion of their child. And "whoever" includes all who stand by and do nothing to prevent the murder of preborn neighbors who live in virtually every zip code. God forgive us. God forgive me.

The prohibition of abortion is not new to the Christian faith, just as it is not new to Scripture. The *Didache* ("teaching") is an early Christian treatise dated to the late first or early second century AD. It takes its title from its first line: "The teaching of the Lord to the Gentiles (or Nations) by the twelve apostles." The *Didache* gives us a glimpse of early Christian teachings. The first section focuses on the twin "law of love," the command to love God and love one another. The second is titled "The Second Commandment: Grave Sin Forbidden." This section outlines the prohibitions of the Law, beginning with murder and adding, "You shall not murder a child by abortion nor kill that which is born."[189] Such practical moral standards, including this ban on abortion and infanticide, "served to distinguish the church from the world around,"

---

[189] Peter Kirby, ed. "The Didache." *Early Christian Writings.* https://tinyurl.com/4e7tb5zc.

observes Carl Trueman. "Christian identity was clearly a very practical, down-to-earth, and day-to-day thing."[190]

Such standards not only distinguished the early church from surrounding paganism, but they also drew many people to the church, particularly women for whom the prevailing culture was oppressive. They may explain why the early church was disproportionately comprised of women.

> The main [reason] is that Christianity offered a more favourable and positive environment for women as compared to the position of women in the broader Greco-Roman world. The favourable environment would have included opportunities for real ministry involvement (with honour and dignity), the condemnation of female infanticide (a practice which had greatly reduced female numbers in the pagan population), fewer marriages with child brides (a practice which was harmful to young girls), lack of abortion (which resulted in greater fertility), and healthier marriages where divorce was condemned and use of prostitutes/concubines forbidden (which also resulted in greater fertility in Christian couples).[191]

The historical evidence of early Christian opposition to abortion is further attested by Councils which not only prohibited it but disciplined those who participated in abortions. Observes Francis Schaeffer:

> In the pagan Roman Empire, abortion was freely practiced, but Christians took a stand against it. In 314 the Council of Ancyra barred from the taking of the Lord's Supper for ten years all who procured abortions or made drugs to further abortions. Previously the Synod of Elvira (305-306) had specified excommunication till the deathbed for these offenses.[192]

---

[190] Trueman, *Strange New World*, 160.
[191] Kruger, *Christianity at the Crossroads*, 36-37.
[192] Schaeffer, *How Should We Then Live*, 222.

If opposition to abortion distinguished the early church from the abortion-permissive Roman Empire, what should the church in America do now? If each abortion is a murder that takes the life of a preborn child created in the image of God, there is no spiritual exertion that is not justified. If loving God means loving our neighbor, then loving God means loving our preborn neighbors who otherwise face death. Passively standing by is neither loving our neighbor nor loving God. It is contempt for sacred, preborn lives stamped with his image. It is a surrender to the darkness.

Lessons may be drawn at this point from the efforts of American Christians nearly two centuries ago who succeeded in the abolition of slavery. Building upon the legacy of William Wilberforce's efforts in the British Empire, these faithful believers relied upon the Bible to set the terms for their work to end slavery. They were vilified in their own time but are heroes in ours. Their biblical strategy has been recast by a new generation who seek to abolish abortion. A similar courage is required now, regardless of what others may think. Future generations will stand in judgment of our action or inaction.

The first lesson is that abortion is a spiritual issue, a gospel issue. It is sin. It is a violation not of any human law but of God's law. It is not resolved by therapy, protests, or excuses but by the conviction of sin, repentance of sin, and forgiveness of sin that comes from the atoning work of Jesus on the Cross. If abortion is relativized, white-washed, or trivialized, Christians undermine the Law of God and short circuit the only forgiveness that is available. And if abortion is a spiritual issue, only the church, with God's help, can bring abortion to an end.

Abortion is an evil with which there can be no compromise. The goal is not to reduce it in the sense of "safe, legal, and rare" but to eliminate it. In the fearless words of Christian abolitionist Harriet Tubman: "Never wound a snake—kill it!" The goal is not to regulate abortion but to end it altogether. The goal is not to make sure that preborn infants with heartbeats are allowed to live but to make sure that every conceived child is allowed to live. The goal is not to reduce abortions in one state but to eliminate them in every state. The goal is not to end abortion with some exceptions but to end abortion with no exceptions. Every healthy child, every Down's Syndrome child, every unwanted child, every child conceived in rape, and every child conceived in poverty is made in God's image. God makes no exceptions, nor should we. The holocaust must not continue.

Abortion demands equal justice. The Fourteenth Amendment, which followed the civil war, established equal justice for former slaves.

> No State shall make or enforce any law which shall abridge the privileges or immunities of citizens of the United States; nor shall any State deprive any person of life, liberty, or property, without due process of law; nor deny to any person within its jurisdiction the equal protection of the laws.[193]

Equal justice grants the preborn the same privileges which every citizen enjoys. If an adult or a born child is murdered, the justice system holds the responsible individuals to account. If a preborn child is murdered, equal justice demands that the responsible individuals—including culpable mothers—are held to account. Anything less is unequal justice and partiality, which God hates.

While the *Dobbs* decision overturned *Roe* and *Casey*, it only vacated a bad decision ("the Constitution does not confer a right to abortion"), leaving abortion law now in the hands of citizens across the country. Writing for the majority, Justice Samuel Alito states, "The Constitution does not prohibit the citizens of each State from regulating or prohibiting abortion. *Roe* and *Casey* arrogated that authority. We now overrule those decisions and return that authority to the people and their elected representatives."[194] In arguing for the neutrality of the Constitution regarding abortion, the majority sidestepped the question of whether the Fourteenth (and Fifth) Amendments (rights to life and equal protection of all "persons") apply to the preborn. This omission means, in effect, that preborn human beings are not "persons."

---

[193] "Fourteenth Amendment: Citizenship, Equal Protection, and Other Rights of Citizens." *Constitution Annotated.* https://tinyurl.com/4mf6fnn4.

[194] Samuel Alito. "Dobbs, State Health Officer of the Mississippi Department of Health, et al. v. Jackson Women's Health Organization et al." https://tinyurl.com/3ks29p87.

Such an understanding is foreign to the Fourteenth Amendment. Legal scholar and former editor-in-chief of the Harvard Journal of Law & Public Policy, Josh Craddock argues that the framers of the Fourteenth Amendment would have assumed its applicability to the preborn.

> I draw on three strands of evidence to support that conclusion. First, dictionaries of common and legal usage at the time of the Fourteenth Amendment's adoption defined the terms "person" and "human being" interchangeably. Thus, the original public meaning of the term "person" included every member of the human race. Second, centuries of common-law precedent and state practice leading up to the Fourteenth Amendment's adoption in 1868 indicate that the unborn were considered legal persons. Third, the authors of the Fourteenth Amendment expected it to protect every human being—especially the weakest and most marginalized. This "original expected application" is indicative of the original public meaning and demonstrates that informed citizens believed that the text of the Fourteenth Amendment applied to every human without exception.[195]

In fear of God, followers of Christ must stand for the dignity of the preborn as full-fledged members of our community, entitled to the same rights and protections that we enjoy, granted to them not by man but by God. If we do not, the deepening darkness will overcome our land. Unopposed, this threat will be America's undoing. With the battle over slavery in view, Abraham Lincoln would warn in 1838 with words as true now as then:

> At what point shall we expect the approach of danger? By what means shall we fortify against it? Shall we expect some transatlantic military giant, to step the Ocean, and crush us at a blow? Never! All the armies of Europe, Asia and Africa

---

[195] Josh Craddock. "A Post-Roe Legislative Agenda for Congress." *Public Discourse* (Apr. 17, 2022). https://tinyurl.com/yutck34k.

combined, with all the treasure of the earth (our own excepted) in their military chest; with a Bonaparte for a commander, could not by force, take a drink from the Ohio, or make a track on the Blue Ridge, in a trial of a thousand years. At what point then is the approach of danger to be expected? I answer, if it ever reach us, it must spring up amongst us. It cannot come from abroad. If destruction be our lot, we must ourselves be its author and finisher. As a nation of freemen, we must live through all time, or die by suicide.[196]

---

[196] Abraham Lincoln. "Lyceum Address." *Abraham Lincoln Online.* https://tinyurl.com/5n7ue4mm.

CHAPTER 5
OMNISEXUALISM

The patterns of homosexuality represent learned behavior which depends, to a considerable degree, upon the mores of the particular culture in which the individual is raised.[197]
Alfred Kinsey

And God said to them, "Be fruitful and multiply and fill the earth."
Genesis 1:28

THE LIE IN THE CULTURE

"San Diego 'throuple' share their story of three dads and two babies."[198] This was not satire nor was it fiction. This was an actual headline from the March 7, 2021 edition of the *San Diego Union Tribune* newspaper recounting the true life, "committed," polyamorous relationship of physician Ian Jenkins, a colleague at the University of California, San Diego. Promoting his just-released book, *Three Dads and a Baby: Adventures in Modern Parenting,* Jenkins describes his homosexual journey to a three-way relationship into which two children were introduced through the process of in vitro fertilization and surrogacy. His journey parallels that of the culture in its rejection of

---

[197] Alfred C. Kinsey et al. *Sexual Behavior in the Human Male* (Bloomington, Indiana: Indiana University Press, 1948), 963.
[198] Pam Kragen. "New Book Chronicles Three Men in a Committed Polyamorous Relationship and Their Journey into Parenting." *San Diego Union Tribune* (Mar. 7, 2021). https://tinyurl.com/2p9ahw2r.

traditional sexual norms, its acceptance of novel sexual relationships, and its deconstruction of the family order. For some, the article prompted dismay, for others, celebration. For everyone, Jenkins' story is a reminder, in the immortal words of Dorothy in *The Wizard of Oz*, "Toto, I've a feeling that we're not in Kansas anymore."

The story actually begins in Bloomington, Indiana in the year 1947, when biologist and sexologist Alfred Kinsey founded the Institute for Sex Research at Indiana University, now known as the Kinsey Institute at Indiana University. Two publications sealed his reputation and defined his legacy, *Sexuality in the Human Male* (1948) and *Sexuality in the Human Female* (1953), setting in motion the sexual revolution that would transform American society. He started by transforming the field of evolutionary psychology, fulfilling the potential noted early by his high school classmates, who dubbed him a "second Darwin."[199] For Kinsey, human sexuality mirrors animal sexuality and can be fully understood in terms of biology and conditioning. "Considering the physiology of sexual response and the mammalian backgrounds of human behavior, it is not so difficult to explain why a human animal does a particular thing," Kinsey writes. "It is more difficult to explain why each and every individual is not involved in every type of sexual activity."[200] This leads to a value-free, permissive, and progressive view of sexuality and a disregard of moral standards as mere "conditioning." Kinsey denies we can judge any sexual conduct as good or bad, moral or immoral. "Whatever the moral interpretation … there is no scientific reason for considering particular types of sexual activity as intrinsically, in their biologic origins, normal or abnormal."[201] This perspective may have appeased Kinsey's conscience in view of his own bisexuality and open marriage.[202]

Drawing upon thousands of interviews and case histories, Kinsey claimed that about one in three married men had extramarital sexual affairs[203] and 69 percent of the total white male population had some

---

[199] West, *Darwin Day in America*, Loc 6193.
[200] Alfred C. Kinsey et al. *Sexual Behavior in the Human Female* (Bloomington, Indiana: Indiana University Press, 1953), 731.
[201] Kinsey, *Sexual Behavior in the Human Male*, 305.
[202] Caleb Crain. "Alfred Kinsey: Liberator or Pervert?" *The New York Times* (Oct. 3, 2004).

experience with a prostitute.[204] He also alleged that "at least 37 percent of the male population has some homosexual experience between the beginning of adolescence and old age"[205] and "only one male in twelve or fourteen (estimated at about 8 percent) ever has sexual experience with animals."[206] Kinsey would famously conclude, in a statement often cited by homosexual activists, that "10 percent of the males are more or less exclusively homosexual ... for at least three years between the ages of 16 and 55. This is one male in ten in the white male population."[207] The validity of these data are widely questioned; his estimates of the prevalence of homosexuality are obviously exaggerated. The research methods used by Kinsey, including interviews of pedophiles, oversampling of prison inmates, and manipulative interviewing techniques, cast a shadow over the ethical integrity and accuracy of his work. Nonetheless, Kinsey's writings were widely read and transformed the country's sexual attitudes, as attested by his appearance on the cover of *Time Magazine* in 1953. Francis Schaeffer summarizes his impact:

> Kinsey made that which is "right" in sex a matter of statistics. Many people read his books because at that date they were far more titillating than other books accepted as respectable. However, their real impact was the underlying conception that sexual right and wrong depend only on what most people are doing sexually at a given moment of history. This has become the generally accepted standard in the years since.[208]

The sexual revolution that Kinsey triggered, informed by his Darwinian worldview, normalized what was once taboo. It removed the stigma that was attached to marital infidelity, homosexuality, and other forms of promiscuous sex. Carl Trueman underscores this aspect of the sexual revolution:

---

[203] Kinsey, *Sexual Behavior in the Human Male*, 853.
[204] Kinsey, *Sexual Behavior in the Human Male*, 870.
[205] Kinsey, *Sexual Behavior in the Human Male*, 908.
[206] Kinsey, *Sexual Behavior in the Human Male*, 977.
[207] Kinsey, *Sexual Behavior in the Human Male*, 949.
[208] Schaeffer, *How Should We Then Live?*, 223.

In short, the sexual revolution does not simply represent a growth in the routine transgression of traditional sexual codes or even a modest expansion of the boundaries of what is and is not acceptable sexual behavior. Not at all. Rather, it is the repudiation of the very idea of such codes in their entirety. More than that, it has come in certain areas, such as that of homosexuality and transgenderism, to require the positive repudiation of traditional sexual mores to the point where belief in, or maintenance of, such views has come to be seen as ridiculous and even a sign of serious mental or moral deficiency.[209]

The battle to normalize once prohibited sexual practices such as homosexuality has morphed from an insistence on the right "to be left alone" to an insistence that all dissent be silenced to an urging that the practice be celebrated. This shift is seen in the now annual Pride Month, the ceaseless promotion of homosexuality by the media, and the legal sanctioning of gay marriage enshrined in the 2015 *Obergefell* decision. It is also evident in work by the educational establishment to influence children to accept, if not practice, non-heterosexual behaviors. First published in 1991, *The Guidelines for Comprehensive Sexuality Education: Kindergarten-12th Grade* developed by SIECUS (The Sexuality Information and Education Council of the United States) has advanced "sexuality education" for use by kindergarten through twelfth grade educators. Its most recent edition includes these standards for Level 1 (middle childhood, ages 5 through 8; early elementary school):

- Touching and rubbing one's own genitals to feel good is called masturbation.
- People often kiss, hug, touch, and engage in other sexual behaviors with one another to show caring and to feel good.
- Differences make us unique.

---

[209] Trueman, *Strange New World*, 22.

- Some people are homosexual, which means they can be attracted to and fall in love with someone of the same gender.
- Telling trusted people about one's feelings and needs is acceptable.[210]

This is not "sexuality education." It is sexual activism, sexual propaganda, and sexual indoctrination. It is sexual grooming of young children by adults to advance a destructive sexual agenda.

The U.S. Centers for Disease Control and Prevention (CDC) is doing its part to groom and indoctrinate the next generation by pointing them to Q Chat Space.[211] Sponsored by Planned Parenthood, PFLAG (the largest LGBT activist organization), and CenterLink (a coalition of LGBT community centers), Q Chat Space promotes itself as "a community for LGBTQ+ teens" that is "safe," "diverse," and "accepting." The site is everything but safe for those as young as thirteen who visit its pages.[212] It directs teens to secretive chats where they can discuss such topics as "Drag Culture 101," "Having Multiple Genders," and "Sex and Relationships." Teens from Christian backgrounds can visit "Q Christian Fellowship," which promises to "cultivate radical belonging for LGBTQ+ Christians and allies." The dark spiritual orientation of the site is revealed by links to "Queering Tarot" and to an astrology chat which asks, "How do your big three astrological signs affect your everyday life?"[213]

The combined effect of these efforts upon sexual attitudes and behaviors would have exceeded Kinsey's wildest dreams. Gallup reports that "the percentage of U.S. adults who self-identify as lesbian, gay, bisexual, transgender, or something other than heterosexual has increased to a new high of 7.1%, which is double the percentage from 2012, when Gallup first measured it."[214] The underlying details of these

---

[210] SIECUS National Guidelines Taskforce. "Guidelines for Comprehensive Sexuality Education: Kindergarten through 12th Grade." https://tinyurl.com/9tfpb5ru.

[211] Centers for Disease Control and Prevention. "Lesbian, Gay, Bisexual, and Transgender Health." https://tinyurl.com/2defyde8.

[212] Q Chat Space. https://tinyurl.com/yckhxwwx.

[213] Q Chat Space. https://www.instagram.com/p/CSo0wzkt6iv/.

[214] Jeffrey M. Jones. "LGBT Identification in U.S. Ticks Up to 7.1%." *Gallup News* (Feb. 17, 2022). https://tinyurl.com/5bbz65nc.

2022 results are even more disconcerting. "Roughly 21% of Generation Z Americans who have reached adulthood—those born between 1997 and 2003—identify as LGBT. That is nearly double the proportions of millennials who do so, while the gap widens even further when compared with older generations." Indeed, the proportion of individuals identifying as LGBT among Generation X (born 1964 to 1980) is 4.2 percent, among Baby boomers (born 1946 to 1964) 2.6 percent, and among Traditionalists (born before 1946) only 0.8 percent. Liberal comedian and social commentator Bill Maher recognizes something about the results is fishy. "Yes, part of the rise in LGBT numbers is from people feeling free enough to tell it to a pollster ... but some of it is—it's trendy."[215]

Maher is right. There is a social—indeed a spiritual—contagion at work, infecting a new generation with fashionable but immoral sexual attitudes. And its spread is not isolated to the culture. It is spreading in the church.

THE LIE IN THE CHURCH

Just as relativistic perspectives on sexuality follow from Kinsey's Darwinian worldview, so, predictably, do the relativistic perspectives of the mainline Christian denominations, who mimic the progressive culture while denying the authority of God's Word. Precisely because the progressive church, in its embrace of evolutionism, has "exchanged the truth about God for a lie and worshiped and served the creature rather than the Creator," God has, in the words of the Apostle Paul, given them up "in the lust of their hearts to impurity, to the dishonoring of their bodies among themselves."[216] Thus the Presbyterian Church (USA) fully endorses the ordination of lesbian, gay, bisexual, or transgender persons, while also encouraging its ministers to perform same-sex marriages.[217] The denomination has added "a

---

[215] Caroline Vakil. "Maher Says Increase in Those Identifying as LGBT Partly Attributed to Being 'Trendy.'" *The Hill* (May 21, 2022). https://tinyurl.com/3n2xt7cr.

[216] Romans 1:24-25.

[217] "What We Believe: Sexuality and Same-Gender Relationships." *Presbyterian Church (U.S.A.) Presbyterian Mission.* https://tinyurl.com/2p8vt8mp.

nonbinary/genderqueer category" to demographic questions asked of its members.[218] The Evangelical Lutheran Church in America has affirmed since 1995 "that gay and lesbian people, individuals created by God, are welcome to participate fully in the life of congregations."[219] The United Methodist Church ordained the first "Drag Queen Pastor."[220] Isaac Simmons, who preaches in drag as "dragavangelist" Ms. Penny Cost in a sacrilegious play on words, has "challenged basic theological concepts, projecting a worldview where divinity rests not in God but in queerness." Simmons speaks of God as "nothing but a drag queen with a microphone of biblical [expletive] proportions." First United Methodist Church in Sherman, Texas even hosted its own "family-friendly drag show."[221]

Others with evangelical roots have jumped on the LGBT band wagon. In his *A Letter to My Congregation*, then Vineyard USA pastor and evolutionist Ken Wilson describes his journey to affirmation of gay, lesbian, and bisexual identities. His route is subjective, informed by "intuition," "discernment," and "Spirit leading" coupled with sympathetic encounters with LBGT individuals. Later, he reinterprets Scripture to argue that biblical prohibitions are not of committed same-sex relationships but of temple prostitution, exploitation of slaves and children, or orgy sex. Conceding that the morality of gay relationships remains disputed in the larger evangelical context, he proposes an inclusive approach to disputable matters according to the "rule of love." "I saw the harm that can result from an over-zealous exercise of exclusion. It's fair to say that I became sensitized, more cautious and sobered regarding the dangers involved in exclusion."[222] He ultimately

---

[218] Rick Jones. "Changes Coming to Church Statistics: Updates Include Adding New Questions, Seeking New Information." *PC(USA) News* (Oct. 25, 2022). https://tinyurl.com/d4zuwznk.

[219] Ann Hafften. "ELCA Youth Spend 'A Day on the Internet.'" *Evangelical Lutheran Church in America News* (May 6, 1998). https://tinyurl.com/ms82jkzj.

[220] Ellie Gardey. "Methodist Church's First Drag Queen Pastor: 'God Is Nothing.'" *The American Spectator* (May 31, 2022). https://tinyurl.com/4xmehpn3.

[221] Gabriel Hays. "Protestors Condemn Christian Church Hosting 'Family Friendly' Drag Night." *Fox News* (May 19, 2023). https://www.foxnews.com/media/protestors-condemn-christian-church-hosting-family-friendly-drag-night-defend-purity-reject-perversion.

[222] Ken Wilson. *A Letter to My Congregation* (Canton, Michigan: Read the Spirit Books, 2016), 88.

advances a gospel reductionism that demeans biblical counterarguments to his own: "The confession 'Jesus is Lord' is not enough, it seems, to hold people together who disagree on this question."[223]

David Gushee, who wrote the foreword to Wilson's *A Letter to My Congregation*, is esteemed as a leading Christian ethicist. A Baptist minister, prolific author, and Distinguished University Professor of Christian Ethics at Mercer University, Gushee is also an evolutionist who works to harmonize the knowledge offered by biblical texts with the knowledge "offered in *stubborn facts* by lives and scientific research."[224] Regarding "Christian LBGTQ people," he asks the church if "we might now conclude that this is one of those cases in 2,000 years of Christian history where we have gotten some things wrong."[225] He appears not to have contemplated the alternative conclusion that the hypersexual present is on the wrong side of two thousand years of correct Christian history. Gushee describes the starting point of his personal transition from a "traditionalist" view of sexuality to an inclusive one:

> My mind has changed—especially due to the transformative encounters I have been blessed to have with gay, lesbian, bisexual, and transgender Christians over the last decade. One of them is my own beloved sister, who is dearer to me than words can say and who came out as a lesbian not long ago.[226]

Like many evangelicals with LGBT family members or friends, "transformative encounters" justify moving the moral goal posts to fit the need. For Gushee, these personal experiences combined with the latest scientific data lead to a revision of his biblical perspective, specifically of how "*not the Bible itself but traditionalist readings of certain texts in the Bible* have become increasingly implausible to me."[227]

---

[223] Wilson, *A Letter to My Congregation*, 55.

[224] David P. Gushee. *Changing Our Mind: Definitive 3rd Edition of the Landmark Call for Inclusion of LGBTQ Christians with Response to Critics* (Canton, Michigan: Read the Spirit Books, 2017), Loc 1435, Kindle.

[225] Gushee, *Changing Our Mind*, Loc 461.

[226] Gushee, *Changing Our Mind*, Loc 313.

He ultimately arrives at the same destination of gospel reductionism as Wilson, a reductionism in which Jesus is remembered for his love of outcasts but divorced from his creative activity as recounted in Genesis.

> But I am suggesting the idea that Christian theology does better leaning forward toward Jesus Christ, his person and his work, his way of doing ministry and advancing God's coming kingdom, the new creation he brings forth, rather than leaning backward to the primeval creation narratives, where we so often run into trouble.

Emergent pastor Brian McLaren sees things similarly, which is why he wrote the foreward to the second edition of Gushee's book. He disparages traditional biblical understandings of sexuality as "fundasexuality," "a neologism that describes a reactive, combative brand of religious fundamentalism that preoccupies itself with sexuality."[228] Here, McLaren has the shoe on the wrong foot; the preoccupation with sexuality is a hallmark of Kinsey's sexual revolution to which biblical Christians are responding, not the other way around. He goes on to reject a "constitutional reading of the Bible" and promotes a revised view of the God of the Old Testament and the Jesus of the New, a synthesis that is long on love but short on truth.

> So if God considers homosexuality a smiteable abomination, sympathizing with the damned takes either a lot of courage or a lot of stupidity. Either way, under the influence of that vision of God, it's much easier to stay loyal to the lucky heterosexual tribe favored by the tribal God ... But if our view of God is transformed by seeing Jesus the crucified as the image of God in whom the fullness of God dwells in human form (as Paul does in Col. 1) and as the radiance of God's glory and the exact representation of God's person (as in Heb. 1), then God has been best self-revealed not in the smiter, but in the one being smitten. In a crucified man, God demonstrates supreme solidarity not with rejecters and excluders, but with the ones who are rejected and

[227] Gushee, *Changing Our Mind*, Loc 303.

excluded, not with humiliators and shamers, but with the ones who are humiliated and shamed. And in that light, it becomes more difficult to cast the first stone at the "sexually other."[229]

McLaren, Wilson, and Gushee are not alone on the slippery slope of LGBT inclusion. In *Deconstruct Faith, Discover Jesus*, Assemblies of God minister Preston Ulmer extols Gushee's devotion to the "deconstructing mind of Christ"[230] (Gushee is also an endorser of his book[231]) and argues that a "big" issue for evangelicals is the "exclusion of the LGBTQ+ community."[232] "One of the things I realized," he admits, "is how compromised people may feel as they reconsider their views on topics such as LGBTQ+, how they read the Bible, and the doctrine of hell."[233] Even celebrated author and pastor Max Lucado has let his biblical commitments slide. After the gay-affirming Washington National Cathedral was criticized for inviting him to speak in 2021 in view of his past comments, Lucado could not apologize quickly enough. "In 2004 I preached a sermon on the topic of same-sex marriage. I now see that, in that sermon, I was disrespectful. I was hurtful. I wounded people in ways that were devastating."[234] While underscoring his belief in "the traditional understanding of marriage," Lucado backpedals: "Faithful people may disagree about what the Bible says about homosexuality, but we agree that God's holy Word must never be used as a weapon to wound others." He takes the same approach as Wilson toward a matter in dispute by suggesting that diametrically opposing views—one the biblical affirmation of traditional marriage, the other the progressive acceptance of homosexuality—can simultaneously be held by "faithful people" in good spiritual standing. Both are in bounds from Lucado's perspective.

---

[229] McLaren, *A New Kind of Christianity*, 179.
[230] Preston Ulmer. *Deconstruct Faith, Discover Jesus* (Colorado Springs, Colorado: NavPress), 98.
[231] Ulmer, *Deconstruct Faith*, ii.
[232] Ulmer, *Deconstruct Faith*, 72.
[233] Ulmer, *Deconstruct Faith*, 83.
[234] David Paulsen. "Max Lucado Apologizes for Past Comments on Homosexuality After Outrage at National Cathedral." *Episcopal News Service* (Feb. 11, 2021). https://tinyurl.com/w6ervz8x.

Plenty of ink has been spilled in production of a new genre of progressive sexuality literature targeting Christians. William B. Eerdmans Publishing Company, for over a century a leading distributor of scholarly and popular Christian books, marked the 2022 Pride Month with its promotion of no fewer than six new LGBT titles. *Family of Origin, Family of Choice: Stories for Queer Christians* tells the stories of fifteen queer Christians and family members who "are as varied as the colors of the rainbow."[235] In *Affirming: A Memoir of Faith, Sexuality, and Staying in the Church*, lesbian Sally Gary "traces the experiences, conversations, and scriptural reading that culminated in her seeing her sexuality as something that made sense within the context of her faith." In *We Were Spiritual Refugees: A Story to Help You Believe in Church*, church planter-pastor Katie Hays shares the story of Galileo Church that "'seeks and shelters spiritual refugees' in the suburbs of Fort Worth, Texas—especially young adults, LGBTQ+, and all the people who love them." There is no shortage of pastors, theologians, bloggers, and authors ready to provide arguments in defense of non-heterosexual relationships and practices.

The LGBT agenda has even made inroads in the contemporary Christian music (CCM) scene. In early 2021, openly queer and Christian-identifying artist Grace Semler Baldridge's "Preacher's Kid" topped sales in the CCM category at Apple's iTunes store. Baldridge describes the album as a "project about coming out as a queer person of faith," adding, "I want to grab the No. 1 spot on the iTunes Christian music chart and claim it for anyone who has been cast out in the name of God."[236] Baldridge reclaimed the top spot later the same year with the album "Late Bloomer" which features the hit "Hallelujah (In Your Arms)," a song the artist describes as an "anthem of queer joy."[237] Baldridge's ascendancy in popular Christian music has coincided with sympathy from mainstream Christian artists for the LGBT cause.

---

[235] "Books to Read for Pride Month." *The Eerdmans Blog* (Jun. 3, 2022). https://eerdword.com/pride-month-books/.

[236] Emily McFarlan Miller. "LGBTQ Singer-Songwriter 'GameStops' Christian Music with No. 1 Christian Album on iTunes." *Religion News* (Feb. 10, 2021). https://tinyurl.com/bddut3an.

[237] Kathryn Post. "CCM Industry Stays Silent on LGBTQ Inclusion as Queer Artists Care Inroads." *Religion News* (Nov. 15, 2021). https://tinyurl.com/yemzyf3e.

Defending her appearance on *The Ellen DeGeneres Show*, whose host is a lesbian gay-rights activist, CCM superstar Lauren Daigle explained, "I think the second we start drawing lines around which people are able to be approached and which aren't, we've already completely missed the heart of God." [238] This veiled response was clarified a week later when a radio host directly asked her if homosexuality was sinful. "I can't honestly answer on that," Daigle said. "In a sense, I have too many people that I love that are homosexual. I don't know. I actually had a conversation with someone last night about it. I can't say one way or the other. I'm not God."

Leading evangelical Christian organizations have also caved to the sexual revolution. The Council for Christian Colleges and Universities (CCCU) and the National Association of Evangelicals (NAE) combined forces in 2018 to back "the addition of sexual orientation and gender identities as categories to federal nondiscrimination law in exchange for religious exemptions."[239] Houghton College President Shirley Mullen, who serves on both the CCCU and NAE boards, wrote in a position paper, "As Christian higher educators, we are increasingly persuaded that the most viable political strategy is for comprehensive religious freedom protections to be combined with explicit support for basic human rights for members of the LGBT community." The Heritage Foundation's Ryan Anderson tweeted in response that "something has gone seriously wrong when the president of a Christian college thinks sexual orientation and gender identity (SOGI) policies are 'basic human rights,' and is willing to trade protection for a real human right (religious liberty) for SOGIs."[240] The CCCU retreat is doubtless motivated by worries that biblical doctrinal commitments regarding LGBT issues could jeopardize federal financial aid under Title IX.

However, the CCCU position is in fact a capitulation to the LGBT-promoting attitudes and behaviors prevalent among administrators, faculty, and students across the landscape of Christian higher education.

---

[238] Jonathan Merritt. "Lauren Daigle and the Lost Art of Discernment." *The Atlantic* (Dec. 8, 2018). https://tinyurl.com/5ef52bxk.

[239] Brandon Showalter. "NAE and CCCU Boards Back LGBT Compromise for Religious Freedom Exemptions." *Christian Post* (Dec. 13, 2018). https://tinyurl.com/2s4apa9e.

[240] Ryan T. Anderson. https://tinyurl.com/nhmxt59c.

Calvin University of the Christian Reformed Church goes beyond the statement that "homosexual orientation is not a sin" to a more identity-affirming pledge "to love our gay, lesbian, and bisexual students" as part of a broad commitment to "diversity and inclusion."[241] "Refuge" at Wheaton College is "open only to Wheaton undergraduate students who self-identify in a variety of ways, including, but not limited to, lesbian, gay, bisexual, transgender, questioning, etc."[242] Azusa Pacific University recently modified its code of student conduct to allow students to engage in "romanticized" same-sex relationships.[243] Others in the holiness, Wesleyan tradition with Azusa Pacific have spoken out in favor of LGBT sexual identities. A 2013 meeting of the Society for Pentecostal Studies on the theme of "holiness"—convening academics from the Church of God, the Church of the Nazarene, the Assemblies of God, and Wesleyan Methodists, among others—featured an address by then president Paul Alexander who "'urged gathered Pentecostal academics to accept "LGBTQI realities" in their churches and seminaries' in remarks said to be 'suffused' with themes of feminist and liberation theologies."[244] This is not altogether surprising as the Society in 2012 scheduled a presentation entitled "Queer Tongues Confess" by Jared Vazquez[245] and continues to tolerate LGBT advocates, resulting in a 2017 cancellation by a host university over speaker Felipe Agredano, "a politically connected LGBT activist."[246]

The shifts in the Christian academy reflect trends in the larger evangelical context. According to the 2014 Pew Research Religious Landscape Study, fully 36 percent of evangelical Protestants believe homosexuality should be accepted, with an even higher percentage among those who believe in human evolution (58 percent), support

---

[241] Calvin University. "LGBT+ Students and Homosexuality FAQ." https://tinyurl.com/nhd8428c.

[242] Wheaton College. "Refuge." https://tinyurl.com/56cw6sed /.

[243] Morgan Lee. "Azusa Pacific Drops Ban on Same-Sex Student Relationships, Again." *Christianity Today* (Mar. 19, 2019). https://tinyurl.com/2s2nr6k2.

[244] Nicola Menzie. "Society for Pentecostal Studies' Presidential Remarks on Race and Sexuality Spark Controversy." *Christian Post* (Apr. 11, 2013).

[245] Julia Polese. "'Queering' the Pentecostals." Juicy Ecumenism (Jul. 14, 2012).

[246] Jeffrey Walton. "Sex Dispute Has Pentecostal Society Scrambling." *Juicy Ecumenism* (Feb. 22, 2017).

abortion rights (54 percent), are politically moderate or liberal (60 percent), do not take the Bible literally (64 percent), or pursued education after high school (61 percent).[247] A 2020 study by PPRI shows that now a slight majority (51 percent) of white evangelicals ages 18 to 49 now favor same-sex marriage.[248]

The wind is certainly blowing to the backs of progressives in the church who are LGBT-affirming. The sexual revolution started by Kinsey in the broader culture has gained steam in the evangelical setting with the support of opinion leaders like Wilson, Gushee, and McLaren as well as the evangelical academy. Members of Generation Z inside and outside the church are increasingly put off by historical Christian doctrine and hetero-normative biblical standards. Perhaps it is time to abandon moral prejudices and cave to the new morality. But they are lying.

THE BIBLICAL TRUTH

The sexual ethics of Scripture are established in the opening verses of Genesis, which sets forth principles and precedents to guide human sexual behavior and attitudes. Genesis, the book of beginnings, tells us of God's perfect design and divine plan for sexuality in the context of man's creation. This narrative precedes the Fall, the giving of the Law, or the perversion of sex that would occur after man's expulsion from the Garden. It sets the standard for what is best and right, good and normal, pleasurable and safe in terms of sexual expression. It defines the sexual boundaries within which people may discover spiritual, emotional, and physical wholeness; it defines the sexual boundaries outside of which people will experience pain, disappointment, sorrow, and death. All precepts for sexual conduct found elsewhere in Scripture are harmonious with the Genesis account, without exception. Therefore progressives, whether inside or outside of the church, seek first to dismantle the authority of the Genesis account of man's creation, since

---

[247] "Religious Landscape Study: Views About Homosexuality Among Evangelical Protestants." *Pew Research Center.* https://tinyurl.com/yjw2mzvt.

[248] "Broad Support for LGBT Rights Across All 50 States: Findings from the 2019 American Values Atlas." *PRRI Research* (Apr. 14, 2020). https://tinyurl.com/4ttyh5zd.

it is otherwise binding precedent. Remove Genesis from the sexual equation and everything is indeed permissible.

The thrice stated fact that man is made in the image of God (Genesis 1:26-27) grounds man's sexual identity in his likeness of God. Sexuality is a holy, sacred thing. It extends from the character and nature of a holy, pure, and righteous God. It is not a merely biological, animalistic, or instinctive aspect of man's nature. It instead encompasses man's spiritual, physical, and emotional totality. It is integral to our loving relationship to God and to one another. The created sexual order is original and unchanging, as applicable today as in the Garden of Eden. It is essential to man's identity and not an evolving aspect of it.

The image of God is reflected in the creation of man as both male and female. This sets the relational context for sexual intimacy—between one man and one woman in the context of a monogamous, lifelong union: "Therefore a man shall leave his father and his mother and hold fast to his wife, and they shall become one flesh. And the man and his wife were both naked and were not ashamed."[249] The oneness between a husband and wife is spiritual, emotional, and physical. This union is consummated by sexual intercourse. The joy and pleasure of marital sexual intimacy is made possible by the physical complementarity of male and female. One does not need to complete medical school to comprehend that their respective anatomies are designed specifically for heterosexual intercourse.

What is right in God's sight also defines what is wrong in God's sight. If the lifelong, monogamous, heterosexual union of a man and a woman is God's stated and only plan for sexual intimacy, other approaches are *not* his plan. The biblical sexual ethic excludes the pursuit of sexual intimacy through all other avenues, including pornography, pre-marital heterosexual fornication, extra-marital heterosexual adultery, pedophilia, incest, homosexuality, bisexuality, polyamory, bestiality, and any other twists that may arise from unrestrained lust. This is a very simple ethic. It is also a level ethic. While a distinction may be drawn between homosexual activity (which

---

[249] Genesis 2:24-25.

is categorically prohibited in Scripture) and heterosexual activity (which is allowed within but prohibited outside of marriage), there is no biblical hierarchy of extramarital sexual sins. They are all deadly. It is biblically wrong to condemn homosexual sin but wink at heterosexual sin. To this point, I share a concern pointed out by McLaren. "Premarital sex is the norm, not the exception, for ... evangelicals as well as other (Christian) brands," he writes. "And it is the norm not by a few percentage points, either—the average 'sexual debut' for an American Evangelical is just after his or her sixteenth birthday."[250] God calls us to be even and consistent in applying his standards of sexual morality to the culture and to the church.

Genesis also explains the purpose of sex. While sexual pleasure is inherent, it is not the ultimate purpose behind God's plan. Instead, God's plan is conveyed in his first command to man: "And God blessed them. And God said to them, 'Be fruitful and multiply and fill the earth.'"[251] Sexual intercourse is a sacred occasion that connects each generation to the next. The purpose of a heterosexual, monogamous union is to conceive children who are birthed, nurtured, and trained by a mother and a father in a coherent family setting. This is God's plan. While God mitigates the realities of unplanned pregnancies or broken relationships, his Word points to what is best for us.

The church cannot influence the sexual behavior of the next generation if it fails to explain the biblical principles underlying healthy sexual expression. Offering a set of rules without an explanatory framework—a coherent worldview—is a recipe for rejection. To say to a young Christian that homosexuality, for instance, is wrong based on an isolated biblical reference is unpersuasive and incomplete. Trueman states it plainly:

> Older Christians can no longer assume that biblical ethics make sense to younger Christians because the social imaginary in which they operate is so different to the one many of us grew up in. And that means we need to work harder at explaining not

---

[250] McLaren, *A New Kind of Christianity*, 186.
[251] Genesis 1:28.

simply the content but also the rationale of Christian morality. [It] is therefore helpful not simply to point to what the Bible teaches in a few texts but also to show that those texts make sense within the larger picture. And this larger picture has both a broad biblical side, where sex is a function of what the Bible teaches about human personhood, and also a "natural law" side, where, for example, the sexual complementarity of male and female bodies is relevant, as is the evidence of damage done to the physical body by certain sexual practices. It is not that nature here offers the decisive argument; yet it does help to show that biblical teaching is not an arbitrary imposition on nature but instead correlates with it. In other words, it assists us in showing that God's commands make sense, given the way the world actually is.[252]

Jesus' teachings go beyond the prohibitions found in the Law of Moses to the more fundamental, spiritual context within which they are best understood. In his most extensive recorded sermon, Jesus explains that he did not come to abolish but to fulfill the Law. When it comes to sexuality, he continues:

> You have heard that it was said, "You shall not commit adultery." But I say to you that everyone who looks at a woman with lustful intent has already committed adultery with her in his heart. If your right eye causes you to sin, tear it out and throw it away. For it is better that you lose one of your members than that your whole body be thrown into hell. And if your right hand causes you to sin, cut it off and throw it away. For it is better that you lose one of your members than that your whole body go into hell.[253]

The prohibition of adultery, from Jesus' divine perspective, is much more than a rule against extramarital sex. It embodies a concern about

---

[252] Trueman, *Strange New World*, 169.
[253] Matthew 5:27-30.

what happens in the mind and in the heart when a man looks at a woman with lustful intent. Jesus knew that such lust is deadly to the spirit and contrary to the law of love. The severity of his remedy, which may be understood figuratively, makes this obvious. Better to amputate the lust now, whatever it takes, than to spend eternity in hell.

The call to follow Christ is a call to self-denial. "If anyone would come after me, let him deny himself and take up his cross and follow me."[254] British pastor Sam Allberry, who has come to terms with his own same-sex attraction, invites everyone to take seriously the call to "take up his cross."

> I am to deny myself, take up my Cross and follow Him. Every Christian is called to costly sacrifice. Denying yourself does not mean tweaking your behavior here and there. It is saying *"no"* to your deepest sense of who you are, for the sake of Christ ... Ever since I have been open about my experiences of homosexuality, a number of Christians have said something like this: "The gospel must be harder for you than for me," as though I have more to give up than they do. But the fact is that the gospel demands *everything of all of us*. If someone thinks the gospel has somehow slotted into their life quite easily, without causing any major adjustments to their lifestyle or aspirations, it is likely they have not really started following Jesus at all.[255]

Paul addresses sexual immorality similarly by placing it in a broader, spiritual context. In his first letter to the Corinthians, he addresses cult prostitution, a common practice in pagan Roman culture.

> Do you not know that your bodies are members of Christ? Shall I then take the members of Christ and make them members of a prostitute? Never! Or do you not know that he who is joined to a prostitute becomes one body with her? For, as it is written, "The

---

[254] Matthew 16:24.

[255] Sam Allberry. *Is God Anti-Gay? And Other Questions About Homosexuality, the Bible and Same-Sex Attraction* (Surrey, England: The Good Book Company, 2013), 7.

two will become one flesh." But he who is joined to the Lord becomes one spirit with him. Flee from sexual immorality. Every other sin a person commits is outside the body, but the sexually immoral person sins against his own body. Or do you not know that your body is a temple of the Holy Spirit within you, whom you have from God? You are not your own, for you were bought with a price. So glorify God in your body.[256]

Paul's understanding of the body as a temple can be traced to Genesis, where God breathed his life-giving presence into the first man, just as his presence filled the temple that stood in Jerusalem. Paul also elevates sexuality above the biological to the spiritual level. Intercourse between a man and a woman, as explained in Genesis, is a union not merely in the physical but in the spiritual sense. This spiritual unity should be a loving one between a man and a woman, both of whom are vessels of God's holy presence, rather than a lustful tryst with a cult prostitute. Sexual immorality violates the presence of the Holy Spirit, who indwells the believer. It defiles his temple. It cheapens the price paid by Christ on the Cross. Contrary to the progressive voices who encourage sexual immorality, Paul's imperative is blunt and urgent: flee it.

The wisdom of Scripture is proven in medical practice. The "sexual history" is a part of each patient's evaluation. Over the years, I have heard just about everything. While some are brazen in their promiscuity, many are ambivalent or regretful. Some bear the medical sequelae of chronic infections, cancer, or physical injury. For others, the relational harm of extramarital sexual activity contributes to loneliness and depression. For most, the spiritual consequences of sex outside of marriage are real and unresolved. For all, my advice remains that the only "safe sex" from a physical, emotional, and relational standpoint is enjoyed within the parameters of a loving, lifelong marriage of a man and a woman.

Early Christian history also lines up with the biblical sexual ethic defined by Moses, Jesus, and Paul. Michael Kruger observes the striking differences between the sexual ethics of early Christians and

---

[256] 1 Corinthians 6:15-20.

those prevailing in Greco-Roman culture, which permitted men a great deal of sexual latitude, including extra-marital partners, temple prostitution, and homosexual encounters. Quoting Demosthenes, "We keep mistresses for our enjoyment, concubines to serve our person each by, but we have wives for the bearing of legitimate offspring and to be faithful guardians of the household." "In contrast," writes Kruger, "the ethics of early Christianity called husbands to stay faithful to their wives and prohibited any form of sexual infidelity. For Christians, both husbands and wives were to be held to the same standards of holiness and purity."[257]

The anonymous *Epistle to Diognetus*, written in the late first or early second century, underscores the distinguishing character of Christians' sexual standards in their rejection of abortion and safeguarding of the marital bed.

> As citizens, they [Christians] share in all things with others, and yet endure all things as if foreigners. Every foreign land is to them as their native country, and every land of their birth as a land of strangers. They marry, as do all [others]; they beget children; but they do not destroy their offspring. They have a common table, but not a common bed. They are in the flesh, but they do not live after the flesh.[258]

In the early fifth century, Augustine would observe with alarm an early prototype of the modern Pride Parade. His Christian opposition to this demonstration is close to the surface, further evidence of a consistent biblical ethic over time.

> Concerning the effeminates consecrated to the same Great Mother, in defiance of all the modesty which belongs to men and women, Varro has not wished to say anything, nor do I remember to have read anywhere aught concerning them. These effeminates, no later than yesterday, were going through the

---

[257] Kruger, *Christianity at the Crossroads*, 37.
[258] *Epistle to Diognetus*, 6.

streets and places of Carthage with anointed hair, whitened faces, relaxed bodies, and feminine gait, exacting from the people the means of maintaining their ignominious lives. Nothing has been said concerning them. Interpretation failed, reason blushed, speech was silent.[259]

The Christian sexual ethic endured for two thousand years and was commonly held within the church until the influence of materialism, evolutionism, and relativism finally caught up in the last century. It cannot be restored unless and until the church recovers its respect for the authority of God's Word, its honor of God's creation, its regard for God's holiness, and its love for God's person. Like the early Christians of centuries past, the church must be distinct from the culture in its sexual ethic, not blended with it. The church must take a stance that encompasses both truth and love—truth in identifying the deadly force of sexual sin that leads to destruction and love in proclaiming the redemptive reach of Jesus' Cross. The biblical approach to all sexual sinners—homosexual, heterosexual, bisexual, or otherwise—is captured in this paraphrase of Alistair Begg: "We cannot hate them because of God's Word, and we cannot affirm them because of God's Word."[260] May we love them as Christ has loved us.

---

[259] "Nicene and Post-Nicene Fathers: Series I/Volume II/City of God/Book VII/Chapter 26." *Wikisource.* https://tinyurl.com/27v8extc.

[260] Michael Foust. "Alistair Begg: We Must Not 'Rewrite the Bible' to 'Accommodate' the World." *Christian Headlines* (Jul. 5, 2022). https://tinyurl.com/565webe2.

CHAPTER 6
TRANSGENDERISM

Regardless of genital sexual status, everyone's brain carries a socialized implant of the gender schema of each sex.[261]
John Money

So God created man in his own image, in the image of God he created him; male and female he created them.
Genesis 1:27

THE LIE IN THE CULTURE

San Francisco was the epicenter of the sexual revolution during the 1960s and 1970s. The Haight-Ashbury district was synonymous with the sexual freedom that defined the broader hippie counterculture of "sex, love, and rock 'n roll." This legacy continued in the nearby Castro District where homosexuality was celebrated in the open. In 1964, *LIFE* magazine would dub the city "Gay Capital of the U.S." By the time I attended medical school at the University of California, San Francisco (UCSF) in the mid-1980s, less than a mile from the intersection of Haight and Ashbury and in eyesight of the Castro District, the city's reputation for homosexual activism was secure. However, though UCSF was a world class research university in a culturally progressive

---

[261] John Money. *Lovemaps: Clinical Concepts of Sexual/Erotic Health and Pathology, Paraphilia, and Gender Transposition in Childhood, Adolescence, and Maturity* (Buffalo, New York: Prometheus Books, 1986), Loc 4008, Kindle.

city, its curriculum covered intersex conditions but said little about "transgenderism" during my four years of study. The idea was certainly not prominent in our collective awareness. Neither had it been a part of Kinsey's lexicon when he started the sexual revolution a generation before.

The rise of transgenderism owes its beginning to John Money. A psychologist and sexologist, he was a prolific researcher and author in the areas of sexual identity and the biology of gender. He was a Darwinian evolutionist who approached sexology similarly to Kinsey, viewing sex as the sum of biological, primal, and animalistic urges. Rejecting the religious faith of his parents, Money promoted a relativistic perspective on sexuality; the final judge is the self, to whom everyone else should defer. "For the majority of people, their own sexuality belongs to them as profoundly, intimately, and personally as does their native language," Money writes. "Without it, the self does not exist. Those who criticize it, or disapprove of it, annihilate one's selfhood."[262] In his 1986 book *Lovemaps*, Money justifies and destigmatizes even the most outlandish sexual perversions, which he terms "paraphilias," including amputation fetishes, sadomasochism, and coprophilia (pleasure in feces and defecation). He was an enthusiastic proponent of pedophilia, telling *Time* magazine in 1980, "A childhood sexual experience, such as being the partner of a relative or of an older person, need not necessarily affect the child adversely."[263]

A professor of pediatrics and medical psychology at Johns Hopkins University, Money established the Johns Hopkins Gender Identity Clinic in 1965, which began offering sex reassignment surgery in 1966. It is Money who coined the terms *gender identity*, *gender role*, and *sexual orientation*. He defines gender identity and gender role, which he fuses as "gender identity/role" or "G-I/R," in subjective terms:

> Gender identity is the private experience of gender role, and gender role is public manifestation of gender identity. Both are

---

[262] Money, *Lovemaps*, Loc 864.
[263] John Colapinto. *As Nature Made Him: The Boy Who Was Raised as a Girl* (Toronto, Ontario: Harper Collins, 2000), 29.

like two sides of the same coin and constitute the unity of G-I/R. Gender identity is the sameness, unity, and persistence of one's individuality as male, female, or ambivalent, in greater or lesser degrees, especially as it is experienced in self-awareness and behavior.[264]

Money views gender identity as separate from "genital sexual status" and culturally rather than biologically determined.

> Analogously with the way that native language becomes implanted as a schema in the brain, so also do identification and complementation implant their gender schemas in the brain. Regardless of genital sexual status, everyone's brain carries a socialized implant of the gender schema of each sex, one by identification, and one by complementation. This identification schema carries the label, "This is me." The complementation schema carries the label, "This is not me, it is with whom I interact." Ordinarily, the identification schema, which is postnatally implanted in the brain, makes a conjunction with the erotosexual schema of the genitalia that precedes it, prenatally, and is phyletically preplanted in the brain. Phenomenologically, it is the disjunction instead of the ordinarily expected conjunction of the phyletically preplanted and the socially implanted aspects of the identification gender schema which constitute the fundamental anomaly in the gender-transposition syndromes.[265]

In other words, no one is born with "boy" or "girl" identity. This is simply an identification "schema" that is overlaid upon the brain during cultural maturation. Though the identification often harmonizes with the genitalia, it sometimes does not, leading to "gender-transposition syndromes," or transgenderism.

For Money, the so called "twins' case" became the signature accomplishment of his career and eventually earned him recognition as

---

[264] Money, *Lovemaps*, Loc 5273.
[265] Money, *Lovemaps*, Loc 4008.

"one of the greatest sex researchers of the century."[266] One twin, David Reimer, was diagnosed as an infant with phimosis, a not uncommon narrowing of the opening of the foreskin. The subsequent circumcision was botched, resulting in the loss of his entire penis. His desperate parents turned to Money, who saw an opportunity to test his concept that gender was due to cultural conditioning, not biology. In experimentation worthy of Nazi physician Josef Mengele, Money would destroy a child in pursuit of his pseudo-scientific fantasies by fully transitioning the infant David from boy to girl. The medical and popular media would assure Money's celebrity while concealing the lasting effects of physical and psychological mutilation on the young Reimer. At the age of fourteen, Reimer abandoned his reassigned female identity and, as biographer John Colapinto writes, "reverted to the sex written in his genes and chromosomes."[267] Reimer later recalled his experiences in traumatic terms. "It was like brainwashing. I'd give just about anything to go to a hypnotist to black out my whole past. What they did to you in the body is sometimes not near as bad as what they did to you in the mind—with the psychological warfare in your head." Four years after completing the interviews that informed his biography of Reimer, Colapinto would receive a call from David's father. "David took his own life yesterday. He shot himself in his car. It was a horrible shock to hear that David had killed himself; but I cannot say it was a complete surprise."[268] David's tragic end sealed Money's infamous legacy while foreshadowing the transgender future ahead. Reimer's story capsulizes the core principles of transgenderism that continue to be propagated by progressives in the culture: dissociation of gender and biology; targeting of children; promoting early medical and surgical transitioning; influencing through medicine, media, government, business, and churches; and silencing truth tellers.

Transgenderism is an ontology, a view of human nature, in which gender is not a biological construct but an inner, intuitive, and subjective one that redefines reality. "At the heart of the transgender

---

[266] Colapinto, *As Nature Made Him*, Preface.
[267] Colapinto, *As Nature Made Him*, Preface.
[268] Colapinto, *As Nature Made Him*, 286.

moment are radical ideas about the human person—in particular, that people *are* what they claim to be, regardless of contrary evidence," writes Ryan Anderson, in *When Harry Became Sally*. "A transgender boy *is* a boy, not merely a girl who *identifies* as a boy."[269] Conversely, a man who *feels* like a woman *is* a woman (transwoman) as fully as a woman with two X chromosomes as possessed by our mothers, wives, sisters, and daughters. The assumed gender identity is all encompassing. It justifies the participation of transwomen—biological men—in women's sports, their occupation of women's dormitories, and their sharing of women's bathrooms. On the flip side, it explains how men can menstruate and have babies. Gender is decided by personal identification, not genetics, psychology, culture, or religion. Theologian Carl Trueman underscores the ascendance of transgender feelings over science, reason, and conventional morality.

> If we take the most dramatic developments of the sexual revolution—say, the legitimation of transgenderism—it is interesting to ask what things wider society already needed to regard as normal in order for this to be first plausible and then normalized. The sentence "I am a woman trapped in a man's body" would have been nonsense to my grandfather. Had it been uttered by a patient to a doctor in the mid-twentieth century, the doctor would almost certainly have responded that the patient had a psychiatric problem and that his mind needed to be treated so as to bring its feelings into line with his physical body. Today, the doctor is more likely to respond that the problem is such that the patient's body needs to be brought into alignment with those inner feelings. Indeed, were a doctor to respond in the earlier fashion today, he might well find himself subject to legal action.[270]

Transgender activists have worked tirelessly not merely for acceptance of transgenderism but for the expansion of the transgender

---

[269] Ryan T. Anderson. *When Harry Became Sally: Responding to the Transgender Moment* (New York: Encounter Books, 2018), 29.

[270] Trueman, *Strange New World*, 27.

population through aggressive recruitment of children and teenagers. This has been accomplished through parents, peers, and educators who have fallen under the spell of the transgender ontology. Celebratory "gender reveals" based on prenatal ultrasound findings have been replaced by a gender-neutral approach to parenting that allows the child to decide gender identity later, often with subtle or not-so-subtle pressure toward the identity opposite the innate, biological one. Not surprisingly, transgenderism has been contagious within progressive communities where adults are most likely to influence suggestable children toward transitioning. Television commentator Bill Maher observes:

> If you attend a small dinner party of typically very liberal, upper-income Angelenos, it is not uncommon to hear parents who each have a trans kid having a conversation about that. What are the odds of that happening in Youngstown, Ohio? If this spike in trans children is all natural, why is it regional? Either Ohio is shaming them, or California is creating them. It's like that day we suddenly all needed bottled water all the time. If we can admit that in certain enclaves there is some level of trendiness to the idea of being anything other than straight, then this is not a serious science-based discussion.[271]

The 2015 *Obergefell* decision, in which the Supreme Court gave sanction to same-sex marriage, was an accelerant to the transgender wildfire that has swept the nation. While the relationship between transgender activists and homosexual activists is sometimes strained, homosexuality is a logical antecedent to transgenderism. By making same-sex union equivalent to heterosexual marriage (which it is not), *Obergefell* reinforced the notion that gender roles are interchangeable. This is illustrated by the ludicrous but explanatory equations proposed by podcaster Michael Knowles, where M = male, W = woman; M + W = heterosexual marriage; M + M or W + W = homosexual union:

---

[271] Vakil, "Maher Says."

If M + W = M + M and M + W = W + W,
then M̶ + W = M̶ + M and M + W̶ = W̶ + W,
or simplified W = M and M = W

These equations are nonsense, of course. A man-woman marriage is *not* the same as a man-man or woman-woman union; the former is a family with biological capacity for reproduction while the latter are not a family and are incapable of procreation. Similarly, a man is not a woman, and a woman is not a man. Such equivalencies are as absurd as stating that two plus two equals five. In the words of Winston Smith, the protagonist who rebels against totalitarianism in George Orwell's dystopian vision of the future, *1984*, "Freedom is the freedom to say that two plus two makes four. If that is granted, all else follows."[272] Truth and freedom go hand in hand. Conversely, if the powers that be dictate that two plus two equals five, or that a man is a woman, freedom is jeopardized by the force required to impose such twisted logic.

That is why standing against the transgender movement entails risk and danger. Opposing views simply cannot be tolerated. When Ryan Anderson published his 2018 salvo *When Harry Became Sally*, in which he warns of the risks and dangers of transitioning, the book was quickly banned by Amazon. Abigail Shrier braved similar blowback when she published *Irreversible Damage: The Transgender Craze Seducing Our Daughters* in 2020. She recounts her experience:

> Cheering this book banning, the deputy director for transgender justice at the American Civil Liberties Union tweeted, "Abigail Shrier's book is a dangerous polemic with a goal of making people not trans." And also: "Stopping the circulation of this book and these ideas is 100% a hill I will die on." A professor of English at the University of California, Berkeley, went further, tweeting: "I DO encourage followers to steal Abigail Shrier's book and burn it on a pyre."[273]

---

[272] George Orwell. *1984 and Animal Farm* (Mumbai, India: Sanage Publishing, 2021), 84.

[273] Abigail Shrier. *Irreversible Damage: The Transgender Craze Seducing Our Daughters* (Washington, DC: Regnery, 2020), xix.

Observing the heavy-handed response to voices against the cultural mainstream, Trueman comments:

> And so we have an ironic situation at present: radical individual freedom has led to rather authoritarian forms of social control, from elementary schools that teach gender ideology to Ivy League schools that have abandoned traditional curricula, from workplaces that require sensitivity training on transgender issues to big tech giants boycotting states because of religious freedom legislation passed by democratically elected assemblies, from local school boards pressing ideological uniformity via the rhetoric of diversity to national governments broadening civil rights legislation to protect chaotic views of gender.[274]

The transgender tyranny has completely overrun the academic medical institutions of the United States, where honest consideration of the scientific facts has given way to unquestioning allegiance to the party line, at the expense of each physician's oath of *primum non nocere* ("first, do no harm"). Just as failure to toe the line of neo-Darwinian evolution can be career ending, so too can failure to defend the transgender orthodoxy. "Gender has transformed into a cultlike concept," writes sexologist Debra Soh, "and public knowledge has been overturned to reflect pleasantries that affirm the feelings and beliefs of particular groups. Scientific research is no longer about exploring new ground but promoting ideas that make people happy."[275] From academic research to office practice, any contradiction of the "a man is a woman" lie is expressly forbidden, with grave consequences for those who commit such an offense. For Soh, her publication of a scientific critique of gender transitioning of young children was a career ender. She was shamed, hated, and vilified as transphobic. She observes in hindsight:

---

[274] Trueman, *Strange New World*, 163.
[275] Debra Soh. *Debunking the Myths About Sex and Identity in Our Society* (New York: Simon and Schuster, 2020), 9.

As left-leaning science denial continues to gain a greater foothold in the academy, research challenging progressive narratives has become increasingly precarious territory. It isn't as though scientists are intentionally publishing controversial research findings with the desire to upset and offend people. But the fear of potentially discovering something that hasn't been given the progressive stamp of approval has certainly become a larger factor influencing the types of questions a researcher chooses to pursue or avoid. Contrary to what you might expect, most sexologists (including me) who oppose these winds of political change are liberals.[276]

The transgender activists' signature accomplishment has been its hugely successful campaign to mandate the use of transgender "preferred pronouns." This manipulation of language reinforces the lie by requiring society to endorse identities at odds with biological reality. It compels speech that contradicts the closely held beliefs of devoted Christians and reasonable non-Christians alike. In New York City, the failure "to use the name, pronouns, and title (e.g., Ms./Mrs./Mx.) with which the person self-identifies" can result in a civil penalty of up to $250,000.[277] Policies against using other than the preferred pronoun, or "misgendering," are spreading across university campuses, school districts, government agencies, and corporations. Even pronouncements from the pulpit challenging the pronoun rules invite blowback. When Pastor Gary Hamrick spoke in defense of a teacher in his congregation who refused to use pronouns in affirmation of his students' trans identities, the local school board fired back: "We call on Pastor Gary Hamrick to recant his allegations due to the libelous and inflammatory nature of the remarks. Unfounded statements such as these not only hurt our community that he is meant to serve but have dangerous ramifications for the incitement of violence."[278] To the heavy-handed

---

[276] Soh, *The End of Gender*, 3.
[277] "Gender Identity/Gender Expression: Legal Enforcement Guidance." *NYC Human Rights.* https://tinyurl.com/mry8fv8z.
[278] Amanda Prestigiacomo. "VA Democrats Target Pastor of Teacher Put on Leave for Refusing To Affirm Kids' 'Trans Identity.'" *The Daily Wire* (May 31, 2021).

efforts of cultural elites to impose transgenderism on the broader culture, author Andrew Klavan responds:

> There are the morally stunted perverts at the highest levels of education and government who want to butcher and drug children out of their God-given sex to bolster a theory of transgenderism that has zero scientific basis and so little logic that it can only be defended by silencing and deplatforming anyone who dares to speak the obvious truth.[279]

Nonetheless, this aggressive approach of silencing and deplatforming over the use of preferred pronouns is working. When asked, "Do you think that kids should be able to pick their pronouns—he, she, or they—or do you think they should be called by their sex," most democrats (61 percent), younger individuals between ages 18 and 34 (56 percent), and urban-dwelling adults (53 percent) believe kids should be allowed to choose.[280]

What is the net impact upon children, teenagers, and young adults who are vulnerable to these social influences? Using data from the Center for Disease Control's Behavior Risk Factor Surveillance System (BRFSS) and Youth Risk Behavior Survey (YRBS), researchers at the University of California, Los Angeles offer updated population data regarding transgenderism in their 2022 study. Nationwide, over 1.6 million adults (ages 18 and older) and youth (ages 13 to 17) identify as transgender, or 0.6 percent of the population.[281] The proportion of U.S. adults who are transgender is 0.5 percent, while the proportion is higher for youth at 1.4 percent, showing that transgender individuals are younger on average than the general U.S. population. There are large regional variations, with 3.0 percent of youth identifying as transgender in New York but only 0.2 percent in Missouri, for the cultural reasons

---

https://tinyurl.com/mrvkn73z.

[279] Andrew Klavan. "Andrew Klavan LIVE at YAF National Conservative Students Conference." https://tinyurl.com/y8czfynp.

[280] "Approval and Mood of Country." *Harvard CAPS Harris Poll.* https://tinyurl.com/243zpvyy.

[281] Jody Herman et al. "How Many Adults and Youth Identify as Transgender in the United States." https://tinyurl.com/2v29p8ca.

highlighted by Maher. Importantly, the number of transgender youths in the U.S. has nearly doubled since 2017.

The attitudes of the American public are also evolving. Updated data published by the Pew Research Center in 2022 finds that most U.S. adults (60 percent) say gender is determined by sex assigned at birth. However, the majority in specific subgroups believe gender can differ from sex, including young adults between ages 18 and 29 (50 percent) and democrat/leaning democrat (61 percent). More respondents credit science with deciding their attitudes about transgenderism (62 percent) than religion (41 percent).[282]

These trends promise more rather than fewer transgender individuals in the future and suggest that the problem is not disappearing anytime soon. They also invite the obvious question: what will be the identity crisis of the future? No one can say for sure. The next abyss may be "transableism," an advocacy term for a psychiatric condition (body integrity identity disorder, or BIID) that harnesses "the stunning cultural power of gender ideology to the cause of allowing doctors to 'treat' BIID patients by amputating healthy limbs, snipping spinal cords, or destroying eyesight."[283] Or it may be the "species dysphoria" claimed by a growing number of people who believe they are dogs, cats, birds, wolves, or even cheetahs. So goes the story of David Benaron.

> He's "a biochemist, inventor, and entrepreneur. He studied at Harvard and MIT, taught at Stanford, and has founded and served in the C-suites of multiple biotech companies. He developed the sensor that enables heart rate monitoring on wearables like smart watches and has made advances in the field of optical blood-oxygen monitoring as well." At the same time, he "assumed the name Spottacus in the 90s, joining the then-fledgling furry community. At his friends' suggestion, he attended his first furry convention, Further Confusion, in the early eighties. He has since been active in furry communities. He chose the name 'Spottacus'

---

[282] Kim Parker et al. "Americans' Complex Views on Gender Identity and Transgender Issues." *Pew Research Center* (Jun. 28, 2022). https://tinyurl.com/4u3jm9z4.

[283] Wesley J. Smith. "End of the Road for Radical Individual 'Re-Creationism'? Not So Fast." *Evolution News & Science Today* (Jan. 31, 2023). https://tinyurl.com/3949jbpm.

as a play on the name 'Spartacus' said in a Brooklyn accent, and because he tends to favor spotted cats."[284]

THE LIE IN THE CHURCH

The Psalmist writes, "I hate the double-minded, but I love your law," reminding us that the perimeter of lawful human conduct is marked by God's commands, no matter the shifting attitudes and erratic behaviors of others.[285] When it comes to attitudes toward homosexuality, bisexuality, and queerness, progressives in the church are truly double-minded. One wonders if anything in reference to human sexuality is out of bounds for progressives. Apparently, nothing is, as their denial of reality and approval of transgenderism attests. Everything is permissible.

Expectedly, the historic denominations, who long ago threw in their lot with Darwinian evolution, have continued down the path of relativism to full-fledged transgender inclusion. As early as 2015, Pew Research Center classified the Presbyterian Church (USA), Evangelical Lutheran Church in America, and United Methodist Church as supporting transgender inclusion.[286] The Advocacy Committee for Women's Concerns of the Presbyterian Church (USA) argues that "the PC(USA) is compelled to celebrate and support transgender ... youth and their parents within our denomination and beyond" against "the rash of transphobic and homophobic legislation being introduced and passed across the United States."[287] They express pride "to belong to a denomination that celebrates gender diversity, recognizing that each person is a unique and beautiful reflection of the very image of our Creator." The United Methodist Church appointed its first transgender deacon, named "M," in 2017. At the commissioning, the bishop prayed a traditional prayer but updated it to include new pronouns. "Pour out

---

[284] Michael Brown. "The Professor and Inventor Who Identifies as a Cheetah Named 'Spottacus.'" *The Daily Wire*. https://tinyurl.com/3949jbpm.

[285] Psalm 119:113.

[286] Aleksandra Sandstrom. "Religious Groups' Policies on Transgender Members Vary Widely." *Pew Research Center* (Dec. 2, 2015). https://tinyurl.com/mjmdxrmk.

[287] Mike Ferguson. "Standing with and Celebrating Transgender and Nonbinary Youth." *Presbyterian News Service* (Mar. 11, 2022). https://tinyurl.com/3uwpb8sx.

your Holy Spirit on M," the bishop said. "Send *them* now to proclaim the good news of Jesus Christ, to announce the reign of God, and to equip the church for ministry."[288]

The Evangelical Lutheran Church in America went a step further, appointing its first transgender bishop, Megan Rohrer, in 2021. In a ceremony fittingly held in San Francisco, Rohrer said, "I step into this role because a diverse community of Lutherans in Northern California and Nevada prayerfully and thoughtfully voted to do a historic thing. My installation will celebrate all that is possible when we trust God to shepherd us forward."[289] Rohrer, a man (transwoman), also uses the pronoun "they" and speaks of love at the bottom of it all: "But mostly, if you'll let me, and I think you will, my hope is to love you and beyond that, to love what you love." Ironically, Rohrer's woke tenure would be cut short in 2022 when he resigned because of "the constant misinformation, bullying, and harassment" stemming from racist allegations made against him.[290]

There is no better indicator of gender confusion within mainstream Christian traditions than the recent announcement from the Anglican wing of the church that there is "no official definition" of a woman. The *Telegraph* reports, "Senior bishops have insisted that until recently, the answer to questions such as what constitutes a woman were thought to be self-evident." Now, however, "additional care" is needed."[291] The issue came to the fore when a lay member of the church asked, "What is the Church of England's definition of a woman?", to which Dr. Robert Innes, the Bishop of Europe, said that "there is no official definition." In one statement, the learned bishop erased the witness of both biology and the Bible.

Evangelicals—and once evangelicals—have worked hard to keep pace. Then Vineyard USA pastor Ken Wilson reflects upon the "jarring

---

[288] Julie Zauzmer. "The United Methodist Church Has Appointed a Transgender Deacon." *The Washington Post* (Jun. 7, 2017). https://tinyurl.com/2s3e5mac.

[289] "Transgender Bishop Steps into Historic Role in The Evangelical Lutheran Church. *NPR* (Sep. 11, 2021). https://tinyurl.com/3yk35ajx.

[290] John Hefti. "Transgender Lutheran Bishop Resigns Over Racism Allegations." *NBC News* (Jun. 8, 2022). https://tinyurl.com/k42npkke.

[291] Kaya Burgess. "Church Has No 'Official Definition' of a Woman, Says Bishop." *The Sunday Times* (Jul. 24, 2022). https://tinyurl.com/59j4yz3z.

introduction to this complexity" when he first met a transman who was a newly baptized believer. Wilson draws an analogy to the biblical treatment of eunuchs, who were excluded from temple worship in the Old Testament but welcomed into fellowship by Jesus and the early church. He concludes that the moral questions raised by his encounter with a transman are "disconcerting" and "not in the 'crystal clear' category," anticipating his eventual full embrace of the transgender ontology as reflected in the subtitle of his book, *An evangelical pastor's path to embracing people who are ... transgender into the company of Jesus*.[292] In recalling this experience, Wilson states, "I scanned my Bible knowledge for help." This scan apparently skipped Genesis, which addresses sex and gender head on. This is to be expected of Wilson, who, as an evolutionist, had already deleted the opening chapters of Genesis from his biblical data base.

Pastor and emergent leader Brian McLaren sees opposition to the trans agenda as just another example of "fundasexualist scapegoating."[293] He grounds his argument in the past use of Scripture to defend slavery (ignoring that the Bible was the foundation for the movement that ultimately abolished slavery), observing that a similar process is at work in the arguments against, among other things, transgenderism. "Yes, we stopped using the Bible to defend certain things once they were 'discredited by events,' but we still use the Bible in the same way to defend any number of other things that have not yet been fully discredited, but soon may be."[294] McLaren expects a day soon when biblical arguments against transgenderism will be as outlandish as biblical arguments for slavery. He then calls for a new approach to issues such as sexuality and gender identity.

> Our quest for a new kind of Christianity requires a new, more mature and responsible approach to the Bible. We pursue this new approach to the Bible not out of a capitulation to "moral relativism," as some critics will no doubt accuse, but because of a

---

[292] Wilson, *Letter to my Congregation*, 38.
[293] McLaren, *A New Kind of Christianity*, 175.
[294] McLaren, *A New Kind of Christianity*, 76.

passion for the biblical values of goodness and justice. Our goal is not to lower our moral standards, but rather raise them by facing and repenting of habits of the mind and heart that harmed human beings and dishonored God in the past.[295]

McLaren is capitulating while stating that he is not capitulating. His eloquence is inadequate to the task.

David Gushee acknowledges that the first chapters of Genesis speak directly to the matter of sex, gender, and identity. He then pivots to the "stubborn facts," including that transgenderism is "embodied by real people." In view of this, he wonders, "How are we to integrate these stubborn facts with Scripture, while responding compassionately to the real human beings in front of us?" Gushee proposes a hybrid third way.

> The third is to find some way to integrate both kinds of knowledge, as many Christians have previously done in relation to a heliocentric solar system and some kind of evolutionary process over billions of years. A simple way to bring such integration is to say that normally, gender identity is clearly male or female and that normally, gender identity matches gender assignment and that normally, sexual orientation is heterosexual. That is to say, this is statistically what most people experience, and thus the way that most societies have structured their marital, sexual and familial expectations, and thus the account most likely to be reflected in ancient religious texts, including the Bible. But it is a stubborn fact that difference also exists in the human family, and not just in the area of sexuality, and not just recently. That small minority of people whose gender identity and sexual orientation turn out to be something different than the majority ought to be able to be accepted for who they are, and assisted, where necessary, in the ways most congruent with their overall well-being. This better reflects the spirit of Christ's ministry than demanding an impossible uniformity and rejecting those who do not achieve it.[296]

---

[295] McLaren, *A New Kind of Christianity*, 76.

Gushee's argument goes like this: since biblical knowledge about the creation of the universe and of life can be discarded in view of the "stubborn facts" of evolution, so also biblical knowledge about gender can be discarded in view of the "stubborn facts" of transgenderism. Put differently, just as Darwin's authority can be placed above Scripture, so also can Money's and Kinsey's. These three are the source points for the "stubborn facts" to which Gushee is deferential. And by rendering one uniformity impossible (that God specially made man in his image, both male and female), Gushee advances another, the transgender uniformity that is being imposed upon society by the power of force.

Christian publishers have collaborated to advance the transgender narrative. Eerdmans' celebration of Pride Month includes Shannon Kearns' *In the Margins: A Transgender Man's Journey with Scripture*, in which Kearns misuses biblical narratives to "make sense of his own identity" and "unlock the transformative power of faith for those willing to listen with an open mind and stand alongside him in the in-between."[297] Brazos Press, a division of Baker Publishing Group, lays claim to Mark Yarhouse's and Julia Sadusky's *Emerging Gender Identities: Understanding the Diverse Experiences of Today's Youth*, which adopts an all-things-to-all-people approach that discounts the Bible ("we do not see much explicit guidance from Scripture on the topic of gender dysphoria or specific interventions"[298]) and embraces strategies that move "toward increasing alignment with a transgender identity," including "more invasive coping strategies, such as medical interventions (e.g., cross-sex hormones, gender confirming surgery)."[299] Among the titles of Cascade Books, a division of Wipf and Stock that "promotes conversation essential to the academy and the life of faith communities," is Vincent Gil's *A Christian's Guide through the Gender Revolution*.[300] A credentialed minister and emeritus professor at

---

[296] Gushee, *Changing our Mind*, Loc 1418.

[297] "Books to Read for Pride Month." *The Eerdmans Blog* (Jun. 3, 2022). https://eerdword.com/pride-month-books/.

[298] Mark A. Yarhouse and Julia Sadusky. *Emerging Gender Identities: Understanding the Diverse Experiences of Today's Youth* (Grand Rapids, Michigan: Brazos Press, 2020), 70.

[299] Yarhouse, *Emerging Gender Identities*, 59.

Assemblies of God affiliated Vanguard University, Gil combines personal narratives, scientific studies, and novel interpretations of Scripture to justify transitioning of diagnosed gender dysphoric individuals who "see modifying the body as a necessary step in freeing them from its interference with identity, devotion, and ultimately their service to God."[301] These are but a sample of the transgender-affirming titles being pushed by Christian booksellers in a rush to be culturally relevant.

Not to be left out, secular publisher Simon & Schuster tracked down the transitioning story of a prominent evangelical, publishing in 2021 *As A Woman: What I Learned About Power, Sex, and the Patriarchy After I Transitioned*, the journey from man to transwoman of Paul Williams, a Church of Christ minister and CEO of a national church-planting ministry. I discovered his book on prominent display at an airport kiosk, of all places. That Williams suffered from gender dysphoria from an early age seems obvious. However, his solution is far worse than his problem, irreversibly altering not only his body but also his relationships with his family, his coworkers, his church, and his God. In his quest for "authenticity," he struggles both spiritually and emotionally: "My heart was demanding to be heard. I was being called to move, to leave the comfort of the meaningful life I was living and embrace the more dangerous life churning within. I was called to transition genders. Paul was to give way to Paula."[302] Along the way, he rejects "evangelical narrow-mindedness" and takes his theology in a different direction. His view of the Creator is muddled: "To me, God is so far beyond our comprehension that I find it easier to define God as the Big Bang, and Something More."[303] His concept of the image of God is also muddled: "I have little idea exactly what that [the image of God] means. What I do know is that when I am preaching, I am in love with God. I am smitten by her beauty, in awe of her otherness, and

---

[300] Cascade Books. https://tinyurl.com/25vukf6w.

[301] Vincent E. Gil. *A Christian's Guide through the Gender Revolution: Gender, Cisgender, Transgender, and Intersex* (Eugene, Oregon: Cascade Books, 2021), 163.

[302] Paula Stone Williams. *As A Woman: What I Learned About Power, Sex, and the Patriarchy After I Transitioned* (New York: Atria Books, 2021), 7.

[303] Williams, *As A Woman*, 148.

confident of her love."[304] With a narcissism that rivals that of gender-confused adolescents on TikTok, he reframes Jesus' teaching on the two-fold law of love—the commands to love God and to love your neighbor—as three-fold, adding, "If we cannot love ourselves, we will never be able to do the other two. That is the theological foundation of our church."[305] Hardly the foundation for any church, this love of self is an unapologetic version of expressive individualism customized to the needs and wants of the progressive church.

These efforts to persuade notwithstanding, most white evangelicals (68 percent) believe that society has become "too accepting of transgender people" while 87 percent believe gender is determined by sex at birth, proportions that have been relatively stable since 2017, according to a 2022 survey published by the Pew Research Center.[306] Still, about one in eight (13 percent) of white evangelicals do *not* believe gender is determined by sex at birth, a belief held by an even higher number of white non-evangelicals (36 percent) and black Protestants (28 percent). Of concern, 29 percent of white evangelicals are supportive of societal trends accepting of people who are transgender, compared to 57 percent of white, non-evangelicals and 68 percent of black Protestants.

The cultural momentum seems to favor transgender inclusion in the long run, both in the culture and in the church. The beliefs and attitudes of the macabre Dr. Money have become mainstream, bolstered by the activism of evangelical elites. Perhaps Money, as well as Wilson, McLaren, and Gushee, are right. Perhaps the stubborn facts of science, the embodied reality of transgender individuals, and the perceived weakness of biblical arguments call for a reassessment of sex and gender. Maybe it is a complex issue that defies easy answers. But they are lying.

---

[304] Williams, *As A Woman*, 149.
[305] Williams, *As A Woman*, 162.
[306] Michael Lipka and Patricia Tevington. "Attitudes About Transgender Issues Vary Widely Among Christians, Religious 'Nones' in U.S." *Pew Research Center* (Jul. 7, 2022). https://tinyurl.com/3cvwce8p.

The Biblical Truth

The first chapter of Genesis provides a definitive and timeless answer to any outstanding questions regarding sex, gender, and identity: "So God created man in his own image, in the image of God he created him; male and female he created them." This summarizes the essential truth about the essential attributes of mankind. Moses reminds us that man is made in the image of God, an image which is constant and immutable. Just as God does not change, neither does the image of God stamped upon each person. The likeness of God is reflected in both male and female. From the moment of conception, as determined by the sex chromosomes (XX in females, XY in males), each person is assigned a sex that is written upon every cell of the body, from the reproductive organs to the brain. While the image of God confers equality upon men and women, the plan of God is unique and distinct for the respective sexes. This pertains not only to procreation but to roles in the family and in society.

God's plan entails both dimorphism and complementarity. Dimorphism indicates that man is created in two, not many, sexes, and that sex, assigned at conception, is not fluid. This is biologically self-evident. Complementarity refers to how men and women are physically, emotionally, and spiritually compatible with one another. This is essential to sexuality and reproduction, as the corresponding anatomies of a man and a woman makes intercourse and conception possible. Humanity has shared this understanding throughout its history, an understanding confirmed by God's Word and proven by observation, experience, and common sense. Without the harmonious functioning of the two sexes, there is no future for any individual, any family, any church, any community, or any society.

The notion of a distinct concept of gender, or the social expression of one's sex, is not native to Scripture, though the biblical narrative allows for differential expressions of maleness and femaleness. For instance, the military record of Israel's defeat of the enemy general Sisera includes the judge Deborah assuming a military leadership role and Jael the Kenite running a tent peg through Sisera's skull.[307] While sex is always dimorphic throughout Scripture, these two women show uncharacteristic combat skill and strength. What the text in Judges, or the Bible elsewhere, does not suggest is that variability or incongruity between the social expression of gender and biologically determined sex ever justifies a change in gender identity.

The equations M = W or W = M are antithetical to biblical and scientific truth. They are lies. This does not disallow that some individuals struggle with a conflict between the inner sense of self and biological sex. In some cases, this is merely a conflict between cultural expectations and individual preferences. In others, it may reflect deeper psychological issues that warrant a compassionate response. Gender dysphoria is real for a very small percentage of the population. As with other cases where subjective perceptions and objective realities collide, the solution is to validate the essential, God-given identity in relation to the subjective perceptions rather than transform the surrounding environment. This is in keeping with what is known from Scripture and from the behavioral sciences: externalizing the problem never resolves internal conflict.

This raises the practical question for Christians: are preferred pronouns a help or a hindrance to those expressing transgender identities? Author and podcaster Preston Sprinkle advocates for the use of preferred pronouns as a gesture of "pronoun hospitality,"[308] an opinion shared by, among others, J.D. Greear, past president of the Southern Baptist Convention,[309] and Wheaton College psychologist Mark Yarhouse.[310] However, such correctness is a full-on surrender to the transgender ontology, betraying a false understanding of both pronouns and Christian hospitality. Preferred pronouns communicate and perpetuate the transgender lie that a man can be a woman, or a woman can be a man. Requiring them compels speech that is dishonest, and dishonest speech is never hospitable. "This wolfish theology cedes

---

[307] Judges 4:4,21.

[308] Preston M. Sprinkle. *Embodied: Transgender Identities, the Church, and What the Bible Has to Say* (Colorado Springs, Colorado: David Cook, 2021), 208.

[309] J.D. Greear. "When Talking with a Transgender Person, Which Pronoun Should You Use?" *J.D. Greear Ministries* (Nov. 18, 2019). https://tinyurl.com/5xshkbe2.

[310] Yarhouse, *Emerging Gender Identities*, 120.

the moral language to the left by using transgendered pronouns as a moral lens ('respect, courtesy, hospitality')," argues Rosaria Butterfield, a once radical LBGT activist who is now a follower of Christ. Its proponents, she concludes, "reject the clarity of the Word of God and replace it with garbage." [311] Obviously, one should not go out of the way to offend a trans-identifying individual. But if push comes to shove, it is neither truthful nor loving for a Christian to use a personal pronoun other than the biological one. As the Apostle Paul urges, "Therefore, having put away falsehood, let each one of you speak the truth to his neighbor."[312] A practical corollary is that Christians would do well not to update their Facebook, Twitter, or email profiles with personal pronouns (his/him, she/her), even when concordant with their biological sex. To do so is to capitulate to the transgender tyranny and the fragmentation of language into meaningless, chaotic subjectivity. Pronouns are not ours to choose; they are conferred at conception by God himself.

For Byron "Tanner" Cross, push did indeed come to shove. A Christian and physical education teacher at Leesburg Elementary School in notorious Loudoun County, Cross ran afoul the local school board when he told them he would not "'affirm that a biological boy can be a girl and vice versa' because he loves children who struggle with gender dysphoria and refuses to lie to them."[313] For this, the school board took disciplinary action, though this was later rescinded after Cross pursued legal recourse. After his victorious hearing, Cross stated, "No government can force its citizens to say things they disagree with. This is especially true in schools, where ideas should be fiercely protected, both for the sake of freedom and the sake of truth."[314]

The truth defended by Cross is both biblical and reasonable. Biblical principles work in the real world; lies do not. In the real world, sex and gender are binary and immutable, male and female. When this reality is

---

[311] Rosaria Butterfield. "Why I No Longer Use Transgender Pronouns—and Why You Shouldn't Either." *Reformation21* (Apr. 3, 2023). https://tinyurl.com/mweknrzn.

[312] Ephesians 4:25.

[313] Prestigiacomo, "VA Democrats Target."

[314] Horus Alas. "School Board Agrees to Settlement on Teacher's Suspension, Legal Teams Spar over Transgender Policy." *Loudoun Times-Mirror* (Nov. 15, 2021). https://tinyurl.com/y3md985v.

violated through gender transitioning, the consequences are also real. The emerging medical literature is filled with conflicting results, some attributable to poor study design, interpretative biases, individuals lost to follow-up, and lack of comparison to other treatment options. Transitioning is not a panacea; it is a nightmare. It aggravates the very mental health symptoms it promises to relieve. Transgender individuals have persistently high rates of suicide attempts (41 percent) and nineteen times higher than average likelihood of dying by suicide.[315] In many instances, the harm could have been averted by leaving individuals with gender dysphoria alone. No fact cited in 2018 by Anderson in *When Harry Became Sally* was more triggering of activists than that gender dysphoria resolves in most children if they are simply left alone,[316] a truth recently corroborated by the chief psychiatrist of Finland's largest pediatric gender clinic, who observes that "it is common for children to strongly identify with the opposite sex at some point in their lives, but four out of five children who identify as transgender will grow out of it during puberty."[317] For those who are not left alone, the therapeutic objective is elusive, since changing genitalia is merely cosmetic. As Paul McHugh, a distinguished professor of psychiatry at the Johns Hopkins University, John Money's home institution, explains: "Transgendered men do not become women, nor do transgendered women become men. All (including Bruce Jenner) become feminized men or masculinized women, counterfeits or impersonators of the sex with which they 'identify.' In that lies their problematic future."[318]

Social media is now filled with the unhappy stories of individuals who regret their medical and surgical transitions and seek to detransition. The themes are recurrent: social pressure to transition, want of emotional support in favor of biological identity, lack of

---

[315] Anderson, *When Harry Became Sally*, 2.

[316] Anderson, *When Harry Became Sally*, 123.

[317] Christina Buttons. "Finland's Leading Gender Dysphoria Expert Says 4 Out of 5 Children Grow Out of Gender Confusion." *DailyWire* (Feb. 6, 2023). https://www.dailywire.com/news/finlands-leading-gender-dysphoria-expert-says-4-out-of-5-children-grow-out-of-gender-confusion.

[318] Ryan T. Anderson. "Sex Reassignment Doesn't Work. Here Is the Evidence." *The Heritage Foundation* (Mar. 9, 2018). https://tinyurl.com/9ezer2an.

informed consent to treatment decisions, failure to offer treatment alternatives, railroading during the decision-making process, financial motivations of treating clinics, poor clinical follow-up post-transition, unexpected and sometimes severe medical and surgical complications, frequent repeat surgeries, persistent or exacerbated mental health issues, loss of sexual pleasure, and deep remorse. These personal stories are powerful since the justification for gender transitioning is subjective to begin with. In the end, those who transition exchange healthy bodies for disfigured ones—breast-less women and penis-less men—that fit their discordant gender identity, while conserving the psychological and emotional problems that prompted the transitions in the first place. In short, gender reassignment is a medical hoax; it is unethical and barbaric. History will not be kind to the physicians who have made and continue to make this butchery possible.

The world of Kellie King was turned "upside down" when, at the age of forty-two, she transitioned from a lesbian woman to a transman, becoming Scott Newgent. She came to realize that the published research is shoddy, that practitioners of transgender care are often sub-par and unaccountable, and that transgender "healthcare" is experimental and dangerous.

> My medical complications have included seven surgeries, a pulmonary embolism, an induced stress heart attack, sepsis, a 17-month recurring infection, 16 rounds of antibiotics, three weeks of daily IV antibiotics, arm reconstructive surgery, lung, heart and bladder damage, insomnia, hallucinations, PTSD, $1 million in medical expenses, and loss of home, car, career and marriage. All this, and yet I cannot sue the surgeon responsible—in part because there is no structured, tested or widely accepted baseline for transgender health care.[319]

However, such sufferings are not what bother her most. It is instead the merciless exploitation of children who are subjected to the same

---

[319] "Interview: Scott Newgent." *GD Alliance* (December 19, 2021). https://tinyurl.com/247he9hp.

torment. "[The] bomb that ignited a fire within me was after I discovered the medical industry was pushing children to transition medically. Once I learned what they were doing to my kids, my profound, relentless nature forged the way to join the hands of disparate groups to fight for our children."

With her book, *Irreversible Damage: The Transgender Craze Seducing Our Daughters*, Abigail Shrier has joined the fight on behalf of children. She documents the way in which gender dysphoria, the diagnostic prelude to gender transitioning, has spread like a virus through the culture, facilitated by peer pressures, social influences, teachers, physicians, and parents. She cites the landmark case of Keira Bell, who petitioned Britain's High Court to review medical protocols which led to her treatment with testosterone and surgical mastectomies, a decision she later came to regret. In 2020, the High Court ruled for Keira Bell. "The court's opinion was damning," Shrier concludes. She describes the High Court's sweeping indictment of medical "Affirmative Care" protocols.

> It noted that the defendant clinic had been unable to explain the sudden rise in teenage girls presenting to the clinic for hormones and surgeries. The clinic had admitted that not a single minor teenage girl had been turned away for inability to provide "informed consent." The High Court noted also that the hormonal treatments came with serious health risks—that side effects might include "loss of fertility" and loss of "sexual function"; that "the evidence base for this treatment is as yet highly uncertain." Finally, the court noted the clinic's own admission that the young women who had begun the process of hormonal transition had shown "no overall improvement in [their] mood or psychological wellbeing using standardized psychological measures." Here, at last, was the first hint that the heavily guarded castle of Affirmative Care might begin to collapse under the weight of so many lies.[320]

---

[320] Shrier, *Irreversible Damage*, xx.

The Court's decision reflects the strengthening medical and legal backlash against the World Professional Association for Transgender Health (WPATH), an activist organization whose standards for "gender-affirming care" drive healthcare policy around the world. Critics of WPATH in the United States cite the "rising scientific skepticism that has led Sweden, Finland, France, and the United Kingdom to retreat" from its "Affirmative Care model," the transgender movement's invalidation of individuals who detransition, and the flawed research used to justify "gender-affirming treatments."[321] However compelling, none of these are *the* reason such treatments should be rejected. *The reason is that they defy God's standards of care and mock the essential nature of persons made in the likeness of God as male or female.* The struggle between the truth of God's Word and the lies of the transgender ontology points to a larger contest of worldviews—a battle over the existence of God (theism versus atheism), the origins of mankind (creationism versus evolutionism), and the nature of morality (absolutism versus relativism).

Arguably modern history's chief opponent of biblical truth is the subject of the next chapter: communism.

---

[321] "Beyond WPATH." https://beyondwpath.org/#declaration.

CHAPTER 7
COMMUNISM

"And you will be like God."
Satan, Genesis 3:5

Therefore the LORD God sent him out from the garden of Eden to work the ground from which he was taken.
Genesis 3:23

THE LIE IN THE CULTURE

A longstanding member of the Communist Party and Soviet operative, Whittaker Chambers would defect from the underground in 1938 and eventually become a writer-editor for *Time* magazine and, most famously, the key witness for the United States government in the "trial of the century" prosecution of Alger Hiss, a high-ranking official in the State Department who was tried for and convicted of espionage on behalf of the Soviet Union. Chambers' courageous writings and bold actions led to the posthumous awarding of the *Presidential Medal of Freedom* by President Ronald Reagan in 1984. In his 1952 memoir, *Witness*, Chambers chronicles his journey from atheistic communism to belief in God, a journey that began with an "inner earthquake" of realization that his communist faith was "evil, absolute evil."[322] In describing his former faith, Chambers traces its origin to the beginning

---

[322] Chambers, *Witness*, 53.

of time, to the Garden of Eden, to the rejection of the Creator, to the rejection of God.

> It is not new. It is, in fact, man's second oldest faith. Its promise was whispered in the first days of the Creation under the Tree of the Knowledge of Good and Evil: "Ye shall be as gods." It is the great alternative faith of mankind. Like all great faiths, its force derives from a simple vision ... The Communist vision is the vision of Man without God. It is the vision of man's mind displacing God as the creative intelligence of the world. It is the vision of man's liberated mind, by the solid force of its rational intelligence, redirecting man's destiny and reorganizing man's life in the world. It is the vision of man, once more the central figure of the Creation, not because God made man in His image, but because man's mind makes him the most intelligent of the animals ... Communism restores man to his sovereignty by the simple method of denying God.[323]

The communist faith was conceived a century before in the mind of Karl Marx, a German materialist, atheist, and revolutionary, who envisioned class struggle as the means of achieving radical equality. This progressive vision is pseudo-biblical in its moral certitude, prophetic zeal, and apocalyptic vision. Friedrich Engels, Marx's co-author of the *Communist Manifesto*, classifies "the whole history of mankind" as "a history of class struggles, contests between exploiting and exploited, ruling and oppressed classes." He anticipates a historical tipping point where the exploited and oppressed classes "cannot attain its emancipation from the sway of the exploiting and ruling class ... without, at the same time, and once for all, emancipating society at large from all exploitation, oppression, class distinctions, and class struggles." Engels expands upon the theme of struggle by connecting historical materialism to Darwinian evolution, concluding, "This proposition [is] destined to do for history what Darwin's theory has done for biology."[324]

---

[323] Chambers, *Witness*, Foreward.

While the American Communist Party succeeded early on in enlisting young intellectuals like Chambers and Hiss, the spread of communism was stalled in the 1940s and 1950s. After all, the "exploited classes" were prospering in the post-World War II period, living comfortably in the suburbs in single family homes with two-car garages. Revolutionary zeal was at low ebb. Then along came Herbert Marcuse. Prior to his emigration to the United States, Marcuse was a member of the Frankfurt School, comprised of a group of German intellectuals who were advocates of critical theory. Concerned by the apathy caused by "a rising standard of living," Marcuse would build upon Marx's call to "a ruthless criticism of everything existing" as an updated means of social change.[325] Marcuse would go on to ruthlessly criticize everything in society to attain through cultural revolution what classical Marxists could not attain through economic revolution.[326] Marcuse's goals are radical freedom, radical equality, and cultural dominance. He summarizes critical theory in Marxist terms adapted to the new realities of the twentieth century:

1. Concern with human happiness, and the conviction that it can be attained only through a transformation of the material conditions of existence.
2. Concern with the potentialities of man and with the individual's freedom, happiness, and rights ... freedom here means a real potentiality, a social relationship on whose realization human destiny depends.
3. The demand that through the abolition of previously current material conditions of existence the totality of human relations be liberated.[327]

---

[324] Friedrich Engels and Karl Marx. *The Communist Manifesto* (Sonnenahalli, India: True Sign Publishing House, 2021), Introduction.

[325] Herbert Marcuse. *One-Dimensional Man: Studies in the Ideology of Advanced Industrial Society* (Boston, Massachusetts: Beacon Press, 1964), 1.

[326] Karl Marx. "For a Ruthless Criticism of Everything Existing." In *The Marx-Engels Reader*, trans. Tucker, Robert C. https://tinyurl.com/yc788bz6.

[327] Herbert Marcuse. *The Essential Marcuse: Selected Writings of Philosopher and Social Critic Herbert Marcuse* (Boston, Massachusetts: Beacon Press, 2007), Introduction.

Marcuse would import these ideas to American universities, first as a member of the faculty at Brandeis University and then, in the 1960s, at my own institution, the University of California, San Diego. Expanding upon critical theory, he argues for the final authority of the self, in line with the expressive individualism described by Trueman: "Our experience always leads back to ourselves ... my experience belongs to me and is inseparable from my being."[328] He anticipates cancel culture and turns the idea of tolerance on its head with his authoritarian concept of "repressive tolerance."

> Freedom is liberation ... it necessitates tolerance. However, this tolerance cannot be indiscriminate and equal with respect to the contents of expression, neither in word nor in deed; it cannot protect false words and wrong deeds which demonstrate that they contradict and counteract the possibilities of liberation ... Certain things cannot be said, certain ideas cannot be expressed, certain policies cannot be proposed, certain behavior cannot be permitted without making tolerance an instrument for the continuation of servitude.[329]

Who, asks Marcuse, is qualified to make "all these distinctions, definitions, identifications for the society as a whole?" "Everyone 'in the maturity of his faculties' as a human being," he answers, "everyone who has learned to think rationally and autonomously."[330] This is hardly reassuring.

Critical theory—the ruthless criticism of everything—has only gained momentum since Marcuse's time. At present, there are critical race theory, critical gender theory, critical legal theory, critical literary theory, critical social theory, critical environmental theory, critical technology theory, and so forth. There is even critical math theory, which recalls the authoritarian insistence that "$2 + 2 = 5$" in Orwell's *1984*. What unites them all is the communist characterization of cultural

---

[328] Marcuse, *The Essential Marcuse*, Introduction.
[329] Marcuse, *The Essential Marcuse*, 37.
[330] Marcuse, *The Essential Marcuse*, 48.

struggle between the oppressors and the powerful—now known as the "privileged"—and the oppressed and the powerless. The privileged oppressors include Christians and Jews, whites, males, heterosexuals, and law enforcement. The oppressed include non-Christians and non-Jews, non-whites, non-males, non-heterosexuals, transgender individuals, and lawbreakers. Among the oppressed, there is an "intersectional" hierarchy based on the number of checked boxes such that a transwoman who is black and Muslim scores highly and becomes culturally dominant by virtue of "lived experience." Toward what end does this critical theory aim? It seeks to overthrow theistic faith, the created order of man in God's image, biblical morality, and the scriptural concept of family in favor of the religion of communism.

Critical race theory is among the most highly developed and socially disruptive areas of critical theory at this moment in time. Much of the credit goes to Ibram X. Kendi, an author and historian who serves as director of the Center for Antiracist Research at Boston University. His best-selling *How to be an Antiracist* is the bible of applied critical race theory. His words and ideas are grounded in Marxist theory and rooted in an apocalyptic vision of cultural revolution. "Capitalism is essentially racist; racism is essentially capitalist," he writes. "They were birthed together from the same unnatural causes, and they shall one day die together from unnatural causes."[331] His language is the language of class warfare: oppressor versus oppressed, powerful versus powerless, victimizer versus victim. Principles of Kendi's critical theory of race may be summarized as follows:

1. Race is "a power construct of collected or merged difference that lives socially."[332]
2. Racism is the combination of "systemic" racist policies and racist ideas that result in racial inequities.
3. Racial inequity is inequality of outcomes.
4. If discrimination produces equity, it is anti-racist.

---

[331] Ibram X. Kendi. *How to be an Antiracist* (New York: Random House, 2019), 165.
[332] Kendi, *How to be an Antiracist*, 35.

5. Assimilation is racist. Claiming not to be racist is racist. "The language of color blindness—like the language of 'not racist'—is a mask to hide racism."[333]
6. "Racism is steeped in denial."[334]
7. Racial struggle is permanent and intersects with other forms of bigotry (e.g., sexuality and gender).
8. The individual is subsumed under the group; guilt and innocence are collective.

Kendi frames race relations in terms of systemic, societal power structures which must be dismantled in their totality to achieve radical equality. This equality is not an equality of opportunity but of outcomes. He cites lower levels of home ownership among racial minorities as an example, seeking not to advance opportunity but to impose equal outcomes so that actual home ownership is identical across races. Kendi's univariate belief that all differences are explained by race is clever, fact-free propaganda. As Thomas Sowell observes, "If there is not equality of outcomes among people born to the same parents and raised under the same roof, why should equality of outcomes be expected—or assumed—when conditions are not nearly so comparable?"[335] Kendi offers no hope of racial reconciliation but only conflict. And there is no relief from the guilt borne by every person in the oppressor class nor escape from the victimhood weighing down every person in the oppressed class.

This sense of collective guilt is reinforced by Robin DiAngelo, an author who writes in the field of "whiteness studies." Her book, *White Fragility*, only intensifies the guilt of her white readers. She agrees with Kendi that race is a social construct, just as gender theorists contend that gender is a social construct. "White privilege" is a system of advantages based on white race; "white supremacy" is a system of domination benefitting whites; "white fragility" is a defensive response to evidence of racism.[336] With Kendi, she refutes the possibility of

---

[333] Kendi, *How to be an Antiracist*, 10.
[334] Kendi, *How to be an Antiracist*, 47.
[335] Thomas Sowell. *Discrimination and Disparities* (New York: Basic Books, 2019), 7.

assimilation and denounces the idea of "color blindness," which "in practice [has] served to deny the reality of racism and thus hold it in place."[337] DiAngelo's concept of white fragility is a version of the Kafka trap: denying being racist is evidence of being racist because someone who is racist would deny being racist. There is no escape.

The pseudo-religious nature of critical race theory is plain. Racism is the original sin exposed by the law of anti-racism.[338] Wokeness represents a spiritual awakening to the pervasive oppression in society. George Floyd and others are not merely victims but martyrs. Oppressed minorities make up the priesthood. Penitence is expressed by unending confessions of guilt. Kendi and DiAngelo, among others, are the theologians. But true salvation is elusive. While perpetual penance may be pursued, there is no final remission of the sin of racism or absolution of the sin of whiteness. The stain cannot be removed.

The religion of critical theory is anti-biblical. It promotes grievance over grace, resentment over forgiveness, and condemnation over love. It offers the veneer of compassion but robs the world of mercy, permitting everything but forgiving nothing in "a world that is not only merciless but Christ-less."[339] Owen Strachan summarizes the crucial differences between biblical Christianity and the wokeness of critical race theory:

1. Wokeness "tweaks the doctrine of humanity, losing sight of the *imago Dei* as our constituent identity."[340]
2. Wokeness "unhelpfully groups people according to 'whiteness,' a deeply problematic concept."[341]
3. Wokeness "actually foments the very sin it presumes to critique: 'racism.'"[342]

---

[336] Robin DiAngelo. *White Fragility: Why It's So Hard for White People to Talk About Racism* (Boston, Massachusetts: Beacon Press, 2018); 2.

[337] DiAngelo, *White Fragility*, 42.

[338] Voddie T. Baucham, Jr. *Fault Lines: The Social Justice Movement and Evangelicalism's Looming Catastrophe* (Washington, DC: Salem Books, 2021), 67.

[339] Mering, *Awake Not Woke*, 26.

[340] Owen Strachan. *Christianity and Wokeness: How the Social Justice Movement Is Hijacking the Gospel–and the Way to Stop It.* (Washington, DC: Salem Books, 2021), 59.

[341] Strachan, *Christianity and Wokeness*, 61.

[342] Strachan, *Christianity and Wokeness*, 65.

4. Wokeness "treats people as 'oppressors' and 'oppressed' due to skin color and power dynamics."[343]
5. Wokeness "traps us in a cycle of anger and victimhood."[344]
6. Wokeness "overturns the Gospel's 'no condemnation in Christ' promise."[345]

What are the dividends of communism, the world's second oldest religion? How well does Marcuse's critical theory work in the real world? Communism confirms an axiom discovered by Chambers as he came to faith in God: "'Man cannot organize the world for himself without God; without God man can only organize the world *against man.*' [The] Communist execution cellars exist first within our minds."[346] The modern experience of communism is unique to the history of the world, as it has organized itself around the non-existence of God. Without God, it has turned the world against man. The millions of corpses left by Mao, Pol Pot, Lenin, and Stalin offer silent testimony. Communists freely use any and every method to achieve their idealistic ends: blackmail, torture, deception, execution, and genocide. The communist world without God is bleak. The vision is utopian; the reality is everything but.

The dystopian reality of communism is becoming apparent in the United States, where the efforts of neo-Marxists and critical theorists are bearing bitter fruit. Identity politics has disrupted social cohesion in favor of distinct factions aligned along the lines of self-interest and pitted against one another. It is a zero-sum game of winners and losers. Cancel culture has executed the "repressive tolerance" of Marcuse to make sure that certain ideas are buried: books are removed from Amazon, curricula are revamped in public schools, history is revised at universities, theology is reformulated in seminaries. Talk of culture wars confirms class struggle is real. The struggle is sometimes violent,

---

[343] Strachan, *Christianity and Wokeness*, 68.
[344] Strachan, *Christianity and Wokeness*, 70.
[345] Strachan, *Christianity and Wokeness*, 79.
[346] Chambers, *Witness*, 55.

as shown by the burning, looting, and killing in the aftermath of George Floyd's death.

A growing sense of unfreedom, of rising tyranny, overshadows the progressive Left's promise of freedom. Inequality is getting worse because of the pursuit of radical equality. "A society that puts equality—in the sense of equality of outcomes—ahead of freedom will end up with neither equality nor freedom," writes Nobel Prize-winning economist Milton Friedman with prophetic clarity. "The use of force to achieve equality will destroy freedom, and the force ... will end up in the hands of people who use it to promote their own interests."[347] Thomas Sowell agrees with him:

> Whether the promotion of separate identities—by race, sex, or other characteristics—is beneficial or harmful in its consequences is an empirical question, and a question almost never confronted by apostles of "diversity." The actual track record of promoting separate group identities, whether called "Balkanization" or "diversity," has been appalling in countries around the world.[348]

The ideas and forces behind the neo-Marxist class struggle tearing at the fabric of our culture are formidable and spiritual, sharing "a bitter taproot that leads all the way down to Hell."[349] They have seized control not only of the universities but of media and entertainment, politics, government, the military, and education. And they are seizing control of the church in their zeal to impose the great alternative faith born in the Garden of Eden, a religion of man without God, a religion of man against man.

---

[347] Milton Friedman and Rose Friedman. *Free to Choose: A Personal Statement* (New York: Houghton Mifflin Harcourt, 1979), 148.
[348] Sowell, *Discrimination and Disparities*, 120.
[349] Metaxas, *Letter to the American Church*, xii.

The Lie in the Church

The evolution of church signage exposes the progressive shift in church culture. In days past, it was common for churches to display the title of this week's sermon, an invitation to Vacation Bible School, a short Bible verse, or an inspirational sentiment such as "Jesus Loves You!" But times have changed. Now it is not uncommon to see messages such as "End Prejudice," "Pride," or "An Open and Affirming Church." Consider this incoherent message prominently displayed by a Congregational Church nearby our home: "There's nothing wrong with loving who you are, she said, 'cause he made you perfect, Babe. So hold your head up girl and you'll go far. Lady Gaga." Some churches signal progressive virtue by announcing the themes of critical race theory with bold clarity: "Anti-Racism," "Black Lives Matter," or "Say Their Names."

Such marquees seem to be more the rule than the exception for the mainline denominations, pointing to an underlying transformation of beliefs and practices. In *Facing Racism: A Vision of the Beloved Community*, the Presbyterian Church (USA) casts a vision grounded in the Marxist notion of class warfare: "The Presbyterian Church (U.S.A.) recognizes that the task of dismantling racism is a long-term struggle that requires discernment, prayer, and worship-based action." The full document touches all the bases of critical theory: "the ideology of White supremacy and White privilege," "racist structures and systems," "race-based system, which benefits some while oppressing others," "dismantling institutional racism."[350] The Presbyterians have been reading Kendi and DiAngelo.

The "Anti-Racism Pledge" of the Evangelical Lutheran Church in America, adopted by its assembly in 2019, is a similar call "to confess the sin of racism, condemn the ideology of white supremacy, and strive for racial justice and peace." The pledge may have been lifted from the pages of *How to be an Anti-Racist*: "I commit ... to become an anti-racist individual in an anti-racist church," "work to dismantle racial

---

[350] "Facing Racism: A Vision of the Beloved Community." *The Office of the General Assembly Presbyterian Church (U.S.A.)* (1999). https://tinyurl.com/bddwvucy.

injustice by listening to voices," and "learn the history of systemic racism in this country."[351] Not being racist is insufficient for congregants and churches; they must become "anti-racist." They are also expected to come to terms with their whiteness by understanding "the ways racism and white supremacy impact every aspect of our life together." Rather than applying the salve of the gospel to racial wounds, the rhetoric of this pledge deepens racial divisions by separating people into warring tribes of the powerful and the powerless.

The United Methodist Church, in its *Stand Against Racism*, sings from the same hymnal used by the liberal Presbyterians and Methodists. It calls for "dismantling racism" as a systemic problem, encoding "anti-racism policies and practices," and ridding "your congregation and ministry settings of all vestiges of institutional racial bias."[352] If it sounds like these efforts are coordinated, it is because they are. They descend from the original communist vision of class struggle, a vision first transcribed by Marx, updated by Marcuse, and contemporized by Kendi. It is a vision that is hostile to God. The progressive church's compromise with atheistic communist ideology is just as unnatural as its compromises with atheistic evolutionism, atheistic relativism, atheistic abortionism, atheistic omnisexualism, and atheistic transgenderism. The long-term results are catastrophic, as these seven deadly lies contest the eternal truth of God's Word.

Though gender theory—in the form of LGBT affirmation—has dominated the critical theory space within the evangelical church, critical race theory has made significant strides. In 2000, sociologists Michael Emerson and Christian Smith published *Divided by Faith: Evangelical Religion and the Problem of Race in America*, arguably the most influential book in the evangelical "wokeness" movement and a study which topped the Gospel Coalition's 2016 recommended reading list on racial division.[353] Drawing upon data collected in the 1990s, Emerson and Smith use the term "racialized society" to capture "the

---

[351] "ELCA Anti-Racism Pledge." https://www.elca.org/racialjusticepledge.
[352] "United Methodists Stand Against Racism." https://tinyurl.com/2tnunsmy.
[353] Strachan, *Christianity and Wokeness*, 35.

meaning of race in America." Their explanation of "racialized society" anticipates the later work of Kendi.

> Not only, we argue, is it a more useful term than prejudice or racism, but it provides a framework by which to guide our inquiry. In the post-Civil Rights United States, the racialized society is one in which intermarriage rates are low, residential separation and socioeconomic inequality are the norm, our definitions of personal identity and our choices of intimate associations reveal racial distinctiveness, and where 'we are never unaware of the race of a person with whom we interact. In short, and this is its unchanging essence, a racialized society is a *society wherein race matters profoundly for differences in life experiences, life opportunities, and social relationships.* A racialized society can also be said to be "a society that allocates differential economic, political, social, and even psychological rewards to groups along racial lines, lines that are socially constructed."[354]

Building on the ideas of Kendi, Emerson, and Smith, evangelical leaders and pastors have eagerly adopted the ideas and language of critical theorists in response to societal pressures and to assuage the sense of collective guilt. That is not to suggest that America—or the evangelical church—is without racial tensions or scarred by the history of slavery. But something is amiss when progress in race relations, evidenced by the twice election of a black president and by the remarkable economic and social assimilation of recent immigrant groups (including newly immigrant African Americans), is erased not by new facts but by new ideology. The ideas of Marx and Marcuse have come of age, dividing and conquering along the way.

The progressive shift of the evangelical movement is apparent in the overhaul of its message in three important respects: the emphasis on attraction over discipleship; the priority of inclusion over holiness; and

---

[354] Michael O. Emerson and Christian Smith. *Divided by Faith: Evangelical Religion and the Problem of Race in America* (Oxford, England: Oxford University Press, 2000), 7.

the insistence on social justice over spiritual transformation.[355] This encapsulates the prevailing character of many evangelical churches as well as the attitudes of their adherents, who, in their eagerness to gain acceptance by the culture, are vulnerable to increasingly virulent strains of neo-Marxist thought. It explains the rapid uptake of critical theories of gender and race. It also explains the displacement of Scripture by progressive ideology, creating a generation of Christians who resemble the culture more than Jesus.

Even before George Floyd, many evangelicals hopped on the racial justice bandwagon by supporting Black Lives Matter (BLM). They did so in conversations with friends, postings on social media, or attendance of BLM-sponsored events. They did so even though BLM is confessionally Marxist, atheistic, anti-family, pro-queer, and pro-trans.[356] One of BLM's cofounders, Alicia Garza, is a graduate of Marcuse's— and my—institutional home, the University of California, San Diego. Her photo is proudly displayed in the University's bookstore, perhaps a tribute to her fulfillment of Marcuse's aspirations for radical social transformation. Her interests include anti-racism, of course, as well as transgender issues. Her revolutionary, anti-capitalist, counter-cultural, and violent dream is emblazoned in her tattoo that reads:

> I am not wrong: Wrong is not my name
> My name is my own my own my own
> and I can't tell you who the [expletive] set things up like this
> but I can tell you that from now on my resistance
> my simply and daily and nightly self-determination
> may very well cost you your life.[357]

That so many evangelicals can march lockstep with BLM activists such as Alicia Garza is baffling. Yes, everyone agrees black lives do matter, as does every life created in the image of God. But no, there is

---

[355] Lucas Miles. *The Christian Left: How Liberal Thought Has Hijacked the Church* (Savage, Minnesota: Broadstreet, 2021), 22.

[356] "Herstory." https://blacklivesmatter.com/herstory/.

[357] Julia Carrie Wong. "The Bay Area Roots of Black Lives Matter." *SF Weekly* (Nov. 11, 2015). https://tinyurl.com/hhcuuwes.

not anything that BLM believes, says, or does that is worthy of Christian support in view of its atheistic and unbiblical roots. Nonetheless, the influence of BLM's brand of critical theory has steadily grown over time. It exploded after George Floyd's death—outside and inside the church. "The effects are obvious everywhere," says Klavan:

> Christian churches hang Black Lives Matter [banners] ... as if they have forgotten that there are no black and white lives in Christ ... It is as if they worship Karl Marx who thought mankind could perfect the world instead of Christ who understood the world is the kingdom of the enemy.[358]

North Central University in Minneapolis, a private Christian institution belonging to the doctrinally conservative Assemblies of God, honored the requests of George Floyd's family to hold his funeral in the university's sanctuary. In his public prayer during the service, its president, Scott Hagan, asked God to "guide this generation to change the national narrative on race and power," framing the event in the powerful-powerless, oppressor-oppressed terms of critical race theory even before the specifics of the incident had been adjudicated.[359] He also announced a new "George Floyd Memorial Scholarship," challenging university presidents across the country to do the same. The institution's website features a now famous mural of George Floyd surrounded by figures with clenched fists—indistinguishable from the clenched fist on the cover of my copy of *The Communist Manifesto*—with the caption "I CAN BREATHE NOW." Another caption, "SAY OUR NAMES," is followed by a list of black people who died in the context of interactions with the police, among them Freddie Grey, Michael Brown, and Eric Garner. While each of these cases are unfortunate, the circumstances surrounding them contradict the implied charge of "systemic racism." The University's messaging parrots the critical theorists in its escalation of racial animus and distortion of facts.

---

[358] Andrew Klavan. "Andrew Klavan LIVE."
[359] "George Floyd Scholarship Fund." https://tinyurl.com/48yratky.

After Chauvin's trial, even Minnesota's leftist Attorney General Keith Ellison would admit, "We don't have any evidence that Derek Chauvin factored in George Floyd's race as he did what he did."[360]

Former San Diego Charger Miles McPherson pastors a large Southern California mega-church that attracts a multi-racial audience. In 2018, he published *The Third Option: Hope for a Racially Divided Nation*, promoting his prescription for racial harmony and reconciliation based on his own experiences of discrimination. While highlighting humanity's sameness in the image of God ("all of humankind shares a genome that is 99.5 percent identical"), he also presents race as "a social construct" and emphasizes racial identities against a backdrop of intransigent racial divisions[361] and persistent white "privilege."[362] He describes ubiquitous "subconscious" tendencies toward racial favoritism, or "othering," manifest not only in "microaggressions" but also "micro-insults," "micro-invalidations," and "micro-assaults."[363] He sees systemic, or "institutionalized," racism as broadly explanatory of disparities in education, healthcare, socio-economic status, and even access to clean water.[364] This patchwork of evangelical faith and critical theory unraveled with news of George Floyd's death. In his sermon the Sunday following, McPherson describes his "sense of powerlessness in a white culture." "I want to say something to all my white brothers and sisters—you have power," he continues. "Can you say that black lives matter—not the organization but the fact? ... Can you say white lives matter? ... That's what the culture says—we get that."[365] This message aligns with Kendi but not Scripture.

Days later, McPherson would express his viewpoint to the nation in an interview with CNN's Anderson Cooper. He begins by highlighting

---

[360] Mychael Schnell. "Minnesota AG Explains Why Floyd's Death Not Charged as Hate Crime." *The Hill* (Apr. 25, 2021). https://tinyurl.com/4wtkej3x.

[361] Miles McPherson. *The Third Option: Hope for a Racially Divided Nation* (New York: Howard Books, 2018), 5.

[362] McPherson, *The Third Option*, 160.

[363] McPherson, *The Third Option*, 174-176.

[364] McPherson, *The Third Option*, 16.

[365] Miles McPherson. "The Third Option: Part 1." https://tinyurl.com/nhabva95. The currently archived version differs from the one originally posted online (and subsequently taken down) from which these excerpts were transcribed.

his book, *The Third Option*, stating, "We honor what we have in common. We have more similarities than differences." He quickly moves on to racial conflicts, "blind spots," and the need for "race consultations."[366] Echoing the anti-racists, he shuns the idea of color blindness as itself racist: "When you say, 'I don't see color,' people are trying to build a bridge, but in fact the person of color just feels like you invalidated everything that they are. This color," he continues, stroking his cheek, "has certain burdens and certain things it's been through, and when you say you don't see color, you're telling someone that you don't see them." He concludes with a call out to former NFL quarterback and race activist Colin Kaepernick, who famously knelt during national anthems to protest the police: "Kaep was kneeling for a good reason. And if we would have heeded his kneeling on the field, we might not be mourning the kneeling on George." Lost in McPherson's rush to judgment are the facts of the case (there is no evidence that George Floyd's death had anything to do with race, as Keith Ellison points out) as well as situational awareness that this false narrative—pushed by leftist radicals—would fuel nationwide riots that would destroy black neighborhoods and businesses.

Only a couple of miles from McPherson's church stands Point Loma Nazarene University (PLNU), the Church of the Nazarene's premier university, positioned atop a high peninsula with a breathtaking view of the Pacific Ocean. It is home to Darrel Falk, past president of BioLogos, who has promoted Darwinian evolution on his own campus and across the evangelical landscape. It is a campus that has been increasingly gay- and trans-affirming, with the support of both administration and faculty.[367] With George Floyd's death, it also steered in the direction of critical theory. Under the banner of "diversity, equity, and inclusion," President Bob Brower led the way in establishing a "Collective on Anti-Racism."[368] In pursuit of racial justice, the Collective recommends "a full-time employee dedicated to diversity and anti-racism" reporting directly to the president, a "new bias reporting webpage," and "an anti-racism

---

[366] "Rock Church CNN 'Anderson Cooper 360 Third Option' 6/5/20." https://tinyurl.com/mpwvpdm9.

[367] "Diversity and LGBTQ Issues at PLNU." https://tinyurl.com/4b6mxn26.

[368] "Updates From the Collective on Anti-Racism." https://tinyurl.com/3ad4pnnn.

course list available to students." Most chilling is the recommendation to find "ways to assess and score commitment to diversity and anti-racism in the faculty rank and tenure process." In the emerging culture of PLNU, faculty are more likely to be penalized for violations of the arbitrary rules of anti-racism than for violations of the timeless rule of Scripture. This marks an advance not of the gospel but of the progressive religion of critical theory,[369] a religion that deconstructs sex and gender to erase the original and inspired beauty of men and women in God's image while exaggerating genetically insignificant racial differences through initiatives to achieve faux diversity, equity, and inclusion. This religion is itself biased and discriminatory since it preferentially elevates one variable of human identity—race—while ignoring myriad others. As psychologist Jordan Peterson notes, a fair reckoning of the factors that may underlie disparities should include not only race and gender but disabilities, socioeconomic status, physical attributes such as height and weight, native language, education, age, marital status, religion, and health status. In so doing, he calculates the total of "diverse" individuals exceeds a very impractical and pointless 15 million.[370] "Diversity and inclusion," in the words of Bloomberg chairman Peter Grauer, "is a race without a finish line."[371]

Initiatives like PLNU's Collective on Anti-Racism parallel efforts at other Christian universities across the country to promote critical theory in both subtle and not-so-subtle ways. In 2020, Azusa Pacific University asked teachers to make a "commitment to read, watch, or listen" to recommended resources on "Allyship and Anti-racism," directing them to a list that includes, among others, Kendi's *How to Be Anti-Racist* and DiAngelo's *White Fragility*.[372] Shortly after George Floyd's death, the president of Biola University addressed the campus community by letter to state that "black lives do matter," while announcing a plan to pursue racial "advocacy" through new "diversity

---

[369] "Anti-Racism: PLNU's Progressive Illiberal Gospel." *The Bresee Collective.* https://tinyurl.com/526pm7kz.

[370] Jordan Peterson. "Jordan Peterson: Why the Western Emphasis on Individuals Is the Ultimate in Intersectionality." *National Post* (Nov. 2, 2019). https://tinyurl.com/2t8rv44j.

[371] Peter Grauer. https://twitter.com/outleadership/status/1256261856966119425.

[372] Megan Basham. "How Woke Interlopers Are Transforming Christian Higher Education." *The Daily Wire.* https://tinyurl.com/mwvfzyyk.

initiatives." Wheaton College held a "Racialized Minority Recognition Ceremony" during graduation and removed a plaque honoring Jim Elliott's martyrdom as a missionary to Ecuador, this because the inscription used the word "savage" to describe his murderers. Even right-wing Liberty University has caved to the pressure, establishing a new department to oversee "equity and inclusion," mirroring trendy departments in universities and corporations across the country that promote inequity and exclusion.

Conservatives and progressives within America's largest evangelical denomination, the Southern Baptist Convention (SBC), are increasingly at odds over racial justice. According to Voddie Baucham, a Baptist minister and Dean of Theology at the African Christian University in Zambia, this "fault line" within the SBC is between biblical justice on the one hand and "critical social justice" on the other. "I believe the current concept of social justice is incompatible with biblical Christianity," he writes. "This is the main fault line at the root of the current debate—the epicenter of the Big One that, when it finally shifts with all its force, threatens to split evangelicalism right down the middle."[373] As evidence that his concern is not exaggerated, Baucham cites the incendiary comments of Matthew Hall, provost of Southern Baptist Theological Seminary:

> Everything that you assumed or thought was normal in the world, or everything you thought was true about your tradition, your denomination, your own family, I'm going to pull the veil back, and what looked like this beautiful narrative of faithfulness and orthodoxy, and of truth and righteousness and justice, I'm gonna peel that back and I'm going to show you the rotting corpse of white supremacy that's underneath the surface.[374]

Hall's self-righteous contempt for godly tradition, faith, and orthodoxy is itself a thin veil covering the rotting corpse of anti-racism. It is hard to imagine the continued coexistence of such antithetical views, which

---

[373] Baucham, *Fault Lines*, 5.
[374] Baucham, *Fault Lines*, 75.

is why Baucham is pessimistic of the long-term prospects of the SBC specifically and evangelicalism generally. Similar fault lines have already split the Presbyterians, Methodists, and Lutherans into conservative and progressive wings. More fractures appear to be on the horizon.

Phil Vischer, the creator of Veggie Tales, expresses his progressivism in a more temperate way than Hall, though no less dismissive of biblical authority. "The Bible can't tell us what it's like to be Black in America, or how to address systemic racism in housing or education. We need to listen to voices who study the issues and have had the experience." Perhaps Vischer is right that the pressing issues of our day are beyond Scripture, better addressed by experts or those with "lived experience."[375] After all, if the voice behind the earnest and trustworthy Bob the Tomato is now channeling Kendi, who knows how to handle systemic racism, it may be time to listen. Perhaps Marx and Marcuse have the real solutions to the intractable problems of the day. Perhaps cultural revolution is necessary to achieve the utopian vision of radical equality and radical freedom. But they are lying.

THE BIBLICAL TRUTH

If the Garden of Eden is where humanity made its first, critical misstep by believing the lie of the world's second oldest religion, "And you will be like God," the way forward is to return to the Creator of the universe, to the Creator of man in God's image, and to the Savior who died and rose again. There is no future without a recovery of the divine order that was lost at the beginning. Man separated from God is lost, blind, and alone. The only option is to seek God again; to do otherwise is folly. It is the folly of all the progressive lies, including communism and its derivatives. It is the arrogance and pride of the fool, who "says in his heart, 'There is no God.'"[376] Karl Marx, Herbert Marcuse, Ibram X. Kendi, and Robin DiAngelo are, by this definition, fools.

---

[375] Baucham, *Fault Lines*, 99.
[376] Psalm 14:1.

If the atheistic premise of communism is foolish, so is the logic that follows from it. If the tree is bad, so is its fruit. "A healthy tree cannot bear bad fruit," Jesus taught, "nor can a diseased tree bear good fruit."[377] The evidence of history is proof that communism is a bad tree bearing bad fruit. To expect a different outcome through repeated social experimentation is folly, fulfilling the definition of insanity attributed to Albert Einstein: "doing the same thing repeatedly and expecting a different result."

If God is sovereign and all the earth is under his dominion, the problems encountered in life must first be seen through a theological lens, through an understanding of our relationship to God. Critical race theory sees all problems through the lens of race; critical gender theory sees all problems through the lens of gender and sex. Both exclude God from the equation; both miss the target. Man's problems and their solution start and end in relationship to God. If this relationship is broken, everything is broken. If this relationship is healed, everything is healed. This was the recurrent call of the Old Testament prophets to wayward Israel. This is the necessity of the Cross, God's plan to reconcile sinful man to himself and to restore relationship with him.

Man's relationship with God determines his relationship to others. When man turns on God, he turns on his fellow man. Fratricide within the first family is proof of this truth. Cain's resentment toward God turned into resentment toward Abel, stoking a murderous hatred. A wrong relationship with God results in wrong relationships with others; a right relationship with God results in right relationships with others. Such restored relationships celebrate our oneness in the image of God, promoting harmony over struggle, unity over conflict, community over tribalism.

What does the Bible have to say about justice? God is both loving and just. If he were only love, he would be permissive and indulgent. If he were only just, sinful man would be without hope. But he is loving *and* just. These twin aspects of his character find their fullest expression in a verse familiar to almost everyone: "For God so loved the world, that he gave his only Son, that whoever believes in him should not

---

[377] Matthew 7:18.

perish but have eternal life."[378] God loved sinful man so much that he sent his only Son to pay the unavoidable, inescapable capital punishment for man's sin. Jesus satisfied not man's sense of justice but God's. It was God's will that he die in man's place. This is the mysterious, incomprehensible, and wonderful reality of God's love for us, without which we would all be justly condemned to die.

Biblical justice is also expressed in God's perfect law. We all appreciate the fact that "traffic justice," the orderly operation of motor vehicles in society, requires traffic laws. Without stop signs, traffic lights, speed limits, and lane markers, the roads and freeways would be impassable. The same is true of man's life in society. Order can only be preserved if laws are understood and respected. The Bible is a communication of God's righteous standards, his moral laws, to which individuals—not target groups lumped together by superficial characteristics—are held accountable. Their observance brings life; their violation brings death. Who is better to define what is best and right than the one who designed and made man in the first place, the one who fathoms man's innermost needs, thoughts, and desires? Of this moral law, Noelle Mering adds, "The very nature of God implies an intelligible moral order of the universe, and denying this order is akin to the denial of gravity. We might be free falling for a time, but at some point, the spiritual physics will cause us to confront the ground."[379]

Communism is lawless because it makes immoral man the center of the universe and the standard for human conduct instead of God. For all its talk of leveling the playing field toward a utopian future of equality, it in fact empowers the few—and the wicked—to impose their will on the many. Stalin comes immediately to mind. Communism pledges freedom but delivers bondage, it claims to be truth but speaks lies, and it promises equality but achieves tyranny. This is always the case when man, without God, is put in charge.

God's perfect law is summarized in two commands: to love God and to love one's neighbor. This captures the interconnectedness of man's relationship to God and his relationship to others. If man loves God, he

---

[378] John 3:16.
[379] Mering, *Awake Not Woke*, 79.

loves his neighbor. If man hates God, he will hate his neighbor. The law of love overcomes the class struggles that are cultivated by communists and critical theorists. It is seen in the Good Samaritan's tender care of the injured Jew by the roadside, Jesus' warmth to the Samaritan woman by the well, Peter's acceptance of the Gentile Cornelius into the family of God, Paul's teaching that "there is neither Jew nor Greek, there is neither slave nor free, there is no male and female, for you are all one in Christ Jesus,"[380] and John's vision of a great, heavenly multitude "from every nation, from all tribes and peoples and languages, standing before the throne and before the Lamb."[381]

The command to "love thy neighbor" has motivated godly people to make a difference in society and to act against injustice. This was the motivation of abolitionists like Harriet Tubman, William Lloyd Garrison, and William Wilberforce, godly people who saw racial injustice and acted out of a loving regard for their neighbors. In this view, there are no racial distinctions. Every man is equal in the eyes of God and a reflection of his image. Slavery is an offense against man and a sin against God that cannot be tolerated. This is very different from Kendi's view that racism may be justifiable if motivated by "anti-racism," that racist people are irredeemable, that the guilt of racism is collective, and that racial conflict is a permanent condition. Biblical Christians ended slavery; communists enslave. The difference could not be starker. Baucham states the facts succinctly: "I have come to realize that culture does matter, that not all cultures are equal, that Christian culture has produced the highest levels of freedom and prosperity and the lowest levels of corruption and oppression in the world, and that transforming culture is a laudable and worthwhile goal."[382]

In the end, the Christian mind, guided by the truth of God's Word, is radically different from the mind guided by human wisdom and deceived by Satan's lies. It is a mind that can only be realized through the transforming power of Christ, who modeled a truly radical and altogether different approach by serving others rather than himself, by

---

[380] Galatians 3:28.
[381] Revelation 7:9.
[382] Baucham, *Fault Lines*, 38.

surrendering his rights rather than claiming them, by giving his life rather than saving it. We do well to emulate Christ. Writes Paul, a man who suffered for the cause of Christ:

> Have this mind among yourselves, which is yours in Christ Jesus, who, though he was in the form of God, did not count equality with God a thing to be grasped, but emptied himself, by taking the form of a servant, being born in the likeness of men. And being found in human form, he humbled himself by becoming obedient to the point of death, even death on a cross."[383]

---

[383] Philippians 2:5-8.

AFTERWARD
BIBLICISM

Your word is a lamp to my feet and a light to my path.
Psalm 119:105

It has been my important though unpleasant duty as a physician to deliver bad news, to inform a patient of a life-threatening condition for which there is no cure. In some cases, it was a terminal cancer, in others, a severe, progressive condition of the heart or lungs. No matter how deeply I sympathize with the patient, it is never an option to withhold the truth. Life-threatening problems need to be handled with candor and honesty. To dismiss the significance of the diagnosis, to conceal the facts, or to ignore the matter altogether would constitute a breach of my professional obligation to the patient. To do so would be neither loving nor truthful.

This book addresses far more serious threats than cancer, lung disease, or heart failure, threats whose implications are eternal. It identifies seven deadly lies which have transformed the culture over the last century and a half, lies told by Stephen Hawking, Charles Darwin, Joseph Fletcher, Margaret Sanger, Alfred Kinsey, John Monday, Karl Marx, and Herbert Marcuse. These individuals have moved society in a progressive, dishonest, and unbiblical direction. Within the evangelical church, their deceptions have been retold by a cast of accomplices, including, but not limited to, Peter Enns, Francis Collins, Ken Wilson, Brian McLaren, and David Gushee. Countless pastors have also done their part—in words spoken and in words left unspoken—to spread the lies of materialism, evolutionism, relativism, abortionism, omnisexualism, transgenderism, and communism. These are the "blind watchmen" who "are all without knowledge" and "love to slumber" during the critical moment of attack, failing this generation as they did Isaiah's.[384] They have all undermined the authority of God's Word by implying the question: "Did God really say?" The consequences are horrific. Only eternity will reveal the full magnitude of the resulting spiritual casualties.

In concern for the present and future generations, the only fitting response is to renew our collective devotion to the Lordship of Jesus and to the authority of his Word. Psalm 119, the longest chapter in the Bible, declares the priority of God's Word as its singular theme, a Word which guides the Psalmist's every step and illuminates his path amid the surrounding darkness: "Your word is a lamp to my feet and a light to my path."[385] It is an ancient expression of biblicism, of allegiance and adherence to Scripture. When Satan is deceiving many, when believers are turning from faith to false ideologies, when churches are slipping off their biblical foundations, it is time to reclaim the eternal, reliable, and authoritative wisdom of God's truth, revealed in the pages of the Bible, from Genesis to Revelation.

The starting point is a personal commitment to God's Word, to hearing, understanding, and obeying its words, in keeping with Jesus' admonition to his followers: "Blessed rather are those who hear the word of God and keep it!"[386] This is accomplished through study, reflection, and application. Aided by the Spirit, God speaks to us directly through his Word, transforming the mind and the heart to reflect the mind and heart of Christ. The discipline of Bible study is essential to spiritual health and growth, just as good nutrition is essential to physical health and well-being. Inadequate intake of God's Word results in spiritual malnutrition, leaving the weakened believer susceptible to temptation and to the attacks of the enemy. The Christian fortified by Scripture can stand strong in the face of temptation. This is the example of Jesus, who, though physically weakened by forty days

---

[384] Isaiah 56:10.
[385] Psalm 119:105.
[386] Luke 11:28.

of fasting in the harsh Judean wilderness, courageously resisted the tempting lies of Satan with biblical truth: "It is written."[387]

The Bible is the key to parenting, to guiding children in a lifelong relationship with Christ and to the eternal rewards of heaven. How can the next generation know who Jesus is if they do not know what he says? Loving Jesus means knowing and doing what he says in his Word: "If anyone loves me, he will keep my word ... Whoever does not love me does not keep my word."[388] Knowing what Jesus says means knowing the Bible broadly. It means discussing *everything* the Bible discusses, from fundamental doctrines such as original sin and the atoning death of Jesus, to hot button topics such as evolution, homosexuality, and abortion. The Bible speaks to them all if given the opportunity to do so. It is comprehensive, timeless, and relevant. To paraphrase the wisdom of Solomon: there is nothing true that is new and nothing new that is true.[389] The Bible was, is, and will always be the *only* book that truly matters.

The Bible must be the centerpiece of corporate worship, whether in congregational or small group settings. The vibrant first church in Jerusalem assembled regularly and "devoted themselves to the apostles' teaching."[390] What did the apostles teach? They taught from the Hebrew Bible, which included the Law, the Prophets, Psalms and Proverbs, and the historical books that together comprise our Old Testament. Today, the church is blessed to have the additional testimony of the Gospels and the Epistles, of apostolic teachings that convey the life and ministry of Jesus and the experiences of the early church. This New Testament is continuous with the Old. Together they are a complete revelation of God's Word. The one without the other is incomplete. This is the tactical reason behind Satan's relentless attack on the early chapters of Genesis. If he can undermine the truth of the part, he can undermine the truth of the whole. If he can deceive people into believing that Christ is not the Creator, he can deceive them into believing that Christ is not the

---

[387] Luke 4:4,8,12.
[388] John 14:23-4.
[389] Ecclesiastes 1:9.
[390] Acts 2:42.

Savior. In view of the integrity of Scripture, the gathered church must engage the breadth and width of the Bible. If Paul "did not shrink from declaring to you the whole counsel of God,"[391] neither should those who teach in the church today. Paul challenges pastors and teachers to something better and higher than the ornamental use of Scripture to top off a cleverly crafted homily or drive home an opinion; he challenges them to exposit God's Word faithfully and systematically, verse-by-verse, chapter-by-chapter, book-by-book. This challenge is given contemporary expression by theologian Walter Kaiser, Jr., who advances a similar standard of biblical preaching: "It must be derived from an honest exegesis of the text, and it must constantly be kept close to the text."[392] The only preaching that is biblical is that which preaches the Bible, the whole counsel of God.

Biblicism is also vital to witness. Paul reminds us that "faith comes from hearing, and hearing through the word of Christ."[393] Christians must bear witness to the word of Christ so that his transforming power can be released in the hearts of sinners. It is not enough to tell unbelievers what they want to hear, or what we think they want to hear, but to tell them the plain truth that they need to hear. Too often, Christian witness seeks to be winsome rather than convicting, dulling the sharp edge of God's Word. When surgery is required, a dull scalpel is not only unhelpful but positively harmful. Anything that hinders the Word from making its clean, sharp incisions is not only ineffective but injurious.

What does biblicism require of us in response to the progressive lies being told in the culture and in the church? It requires something other than silence. Biblical Christians must speak truth in precisely those areas where the conflict within the culture, or within the church, is most intense. Like the workmen under Nehemiah who repaired the walls of Jerusalem, building with one hand while wielding a sword with the other, we must fortify the perimeters of our faith where they are being most fiercely assaulted while brandishing the sword of truth, which is

---

[391] Acts 20:27.

[392] Walter C. Kaiser, Jr. *Toward an Exegetical Theology: Biblical Exegesis for Preaching and Teaching* (Grand Rapids, Michigan: Baker Academic, 1981), Loc 162, Kindle.

[393] Romans 10:17.

BIBLICISM

the Word of God. English author Elizabeth Rundle Charles speaks pointedly of the challenge before us, the challenge before every follower of Christ.

> It is the truth which is assailed in any age which tests our fidelity. It is to confess we are called, not merely to profess. If I profess, with the loudest voice and the clearest exposition, every portion of the truth of God except precisely that little point which the world and the devil are at that moment attacking, I am not confessing Christ, however boldly I may be professing Christianity. Where the battle rages the loyalty of the soldier is proved; and to be steady on all the battlefield besides is mere flight and disgrace to him if he flinches at that one point.[394]

What are the truths which are assailed in our age which test our fidelity? What are the biblical truths attacked by deadly lies told in the culture and in the church? They are seven:

1. God is the eternal Creator of the heavens and the earth—of all matter, time, and space.
2. Man is specially and supernaturally created in the image of God.
3. Truth, revealed in God's Word, is absolute, timeless, and universal.
4. Every preborn life is marked by the likeness of God from conception and deserves the same protection as born life.
5. God designed sexual intimacy to be experienced exclusively in the monogamous, heterosexual, and lifelong union of a man and a woman.
6. God made man in his image as male and female and assigns a sexual and gender identity that is fixed and binary from the moment of conception.

---

[394] Elizabeth Rundle Charles. *Chronicles of the Schonberg-Cotta Family* (New York: Dodd, Mead & Company, 1862), Loc 3842, Kindle.

7. Man in God's image—sharing a common essence that eclipses all divisions and all classifications—can only get along with others if he gets along with God.

In view of the spiritual exigency of our time, when truth is attacked on every front, God calls courageous Christians not to flee nor flinch but to enjoin the battle. He calls all of us to unswerving allegiance to Christ our Creator, Savior, and soon-coming King. He calls us—ministers and laity alike—to an uncompromising devotion to the Bible. He calls us to follow the straight and narrow path illuminated by the Way to eternal life. He calls us to warn those who are deceived by Satan's lies and perishing in the darkness. He calls us to separate from those who tell progressive lies to the body of Christ, whether from without or from within, and to recognize that it is "better to be divided by truth than united in error."[395] He calls us to oppose the false gospel of ungodly diversity and immoral inclusion: "For what partnership has righteousness with lawlessness? Or what fellowship has light with darkness?"[396] He calls fathers bravely to defend their wives, their children, and their homes from the intrusions of the enemy by raising the standard of God's Word in love and in truth. With this standard in view and with eyes fixed upon Jesus, may we be found faithful, obedient to what Christ has commanded us, until the day of his appearing.

---

[395] Adrian Rogers. https://tinyurl.com/2nt9j267.
[396] 2 Corinthians 6:14.

DISCUSSION QUESTIONS

INTRODUCTION

1. What are contemporary examples of Satan's original deception, "Did God really say?"

2. Why do progressive lies specifically target truths defined in the opening chapter of Genesis?

3. How does the progressive church differ from the biblical church in its view of Scripture? Of science?

4. Why do many Christians—and Christian leaders—remain silent when the Bible contradicts progressive lies in the culture?

5. Which is a greater spiritual threat to the next generation: progressive lies told in the culture or progressive lies told in the church?

CHAPTER 1 – MATERIALISM

1. How does cosmology—the understanding of the origins of the universe—shape people's view of God, of themselves, and of others?

2. Why is modern science atheistic?

3. Is it possible to view the first chapters of Genesis as an ancient creation myth and still support the broad authority of the Bible?

4. How do the first ten words of the Bible—"In the beginning, God created the heavens and the earth"—refute scientific materialism?

5. What scientific observations indicate that the universe was caused and designed by the Creator?

Chapter 2 - Evolutionism

1. What is the evolutionary doctrine of common descent and how does it attempt to explain the origin of man?

2. Why is syncretism, exemplified by Israel's worship of both Baal and Yahweh, a fitting word to describe "theistic evolution"?

3. What factors led to the deconversion of Rhett McLaughlin?

4. How is human evolution at odds with the Genesis account of Adam? With the broader teaching of the Bible and the doctrine of salvation?

5. Why is it scientifically reasonable to believe that man is specially created and not commonly descended?

Chapter 3 – Relativism

1. Why do materialism and evolutionism result in relativism and the denial of biblical absolutes?

2. How has Darwinian evolution contributed to the rise of the modern self which assumes the authority of feelings and expects unconditional societal affirmation?

DISCUSSION QUESTIONS

3. From a biblical perspective, what is wrong with Fletcher's claim that "only one thing is intrinsically good, namely love: nothing else"?

4. What does Jesus mean when he says, "I am the light of the world"?

5. According to the Bible, what is the relationship of love and truth? How might this apply when talking to a friend who is engaging in premarital sex (fornication)?

CHAPTER 4 – ABORTIONISM

1. How is the rise of abortion in the United States connected to the widespread belief in evolution?

2. Why is abortion now widely accepted by progressive churches and by many evangelical Christians?

3. Should the murder of a preborn child be treated any differently than the murder of a born person?

4. Is there a moral difference between taking a preborn life before or after it has a heartbeat?

5. Why is abortion a gospel issue?

CHAPTER 5 – OMNISEXUALISM

1. What are the causes of the rapid shift in sexual attitudes and behaviors in the United States such that 21% of Generation Z Americans identify as LGBT?

2. How do we explain the reality that sexual attitudes and behaviors in the church—both progressive and evangelical—mirror those of the culture?

3. What does Genesis teach us about sexuality? Is the biblical sexual ethic applicable to our day?

4. What is the purpose of sex?

5. How would you counsel a nominally Christian friend who is considering a romantic relationship with a person of the same sex?

CHAPTER 6 – TRANSGENDERISM

1. In view of the transgender ontology, what does it mean when a transwoman (man) claims to be a woman?

2. What is a woman according to the Bible? According to the progressive culture?

3. In what ways does the biblical view of sex and gender align with biology?

4. How would you respond to a "non-binary" friend who insists that you use the preferred pronouns "them/their"?

5. What are the risks of "gender-affirming care"?

CHAPTER 7 – COMMUNISM

1. Why does Whitaker Chambers describe communism as the world's second oldest faith?

2. What is the connection between Darwinian evolution and Marx's view of history as class struggle?

3. In what ways does critical theory, "the ruthless criticism of everything," divide people?

DISCUSSION QUESTIONS

4. How would you respond to a friend who invites you to attend a BLM rally? What biblical principles contradict critical race theory?

5. Why is Jesus the solution to the conflict with God and the conflict with one another introduced in the Garden of Eden?

AFTERWARD – BIBLICISM

1. What are the consequences of the seven deadly lies that have spread across the culture and the church?

2. Why is the Bible the only book that matters?

3. What is the measure of good preaching in a corporate setting or good teaching in a small group setting?

4. How should Christians respond when they encounter unbiblical views in their church, in their friendships, in their family, or in themselves?

5. Do your words and your deeds consistently honor and defend these biblical truths?

    - God is the eternal Creator of the heavens and the earth—of all matter, time, and space.

    - Man is specially and supernaturally created in the image of God.

    - Truth, revealed in God's Word, is absolute, timeless, and universal.

    - Every preborn life is marked by the likeness of God from conception and deserves the same protection as born life.

- God designed sexual intimacy to be experienced exclusively in the monogamous, heterosexual, and lifelong union of a man and a woman.

- God made man in his image as male and female and assigns a sexual and gender identity that is fixed and binary from the moment of conception.

- Man in God's image—sharing a common essence that eclipses all divisions and all classifications—can only get along with others if he gets along with God.

ACKNOWLEDGMENTS

The biblical foundations for writing this book were laid by my godly parents and, through childhood and much of my adult life, my pastors, Richard and Elnora Dresselhaus. The Bible preached from the pulpit was also the Bible lived out in our home, where a compelling example of Christlikeness drew both my sister, Ann, and me to follow Jesus at an early age. A passion for God's Word was strengthened by the example of my in-laws, LeRoy and Sharon Bartel, whose pastoral and academic influence have shaped a generation of leaders across the country. Over the years, my faith was nurtured by too-many-to-count saints, who were sound in doctrine and obedient in action. Pastor Melvin Johnson was a bright light during my time in medical school, faithfully sowing the seeds of God's Word in the difficult soil of San Francisco.

A catalyst for writing this book was the encouragement of Robert Menzies, a New Testament scholar, missionary, and friend. Before a word was written on paper, he listened to my formative ideas and convinced me that writing this book would be worthwhile. He has been a mentor through the process, providing input and perspective without which this project would not have come to fruition.

Grant Hochman reviewed the manuscript and detected important opportunities to correct and improve it. His meticulous attention to detail and solid grasp of the subject matter of the book contributed in many ways to its final form.

Most importantly, I am indebted to my wife Shari, who provided unwavering support to me through the process of writing this book. Marrying her was the second-best decision of my life, the first being the decision to follow Christ. With me, she has given top priority to the spiritual formation of our son and daughter, a priority that *Seven Deadly Lies* seeks to safeguard. We have no greater joy than seeing our children grow in the Lord and in the knowledge of his Word, as he directs them in the paths of his choosing for their lives.

ABOUT THE AUTHOR

DR. TIMOTHY DRESSELHAUS is Clinical Professor Emeritus, School of Medicine, University of California, San Diego. He received his bachelor's degree in History from the University of California, San Diego, graduating Summa cum Laude and Phi Beta Kappa, while also winning the Armand Rappaport prize, the History Department's highest honor, for his thesis on Arthur Schopenhauer, the intellectual forerunner to Friedrich Nietzsche. He received his medical degree from the University of California, San Francisco and was elected to the Alpha Omega Alpha national medical honor society. He completed his Internal Medicine residency at the University of California, San Diego, serving an additional year as a Chief Medical Resident before joining its faculty. He earned a Masters in Public Health from the University of Washington, Seattle. His professional career has encompassed healthcare administration, health services research, and medical education. He served as Chief of Primary Care at the VA San Diego Healthcare System and in national leadership roles for the Veterans Health Administration, Washington, DC. Author or co-author of thirty-five research articles, he has been a Principal Investigator, Co-Principal Investigator, or Co-Investigator on multiple funded research projects. He has served as a teacher, elder, and musician in his local church and in national leadership roles related to world missions, as a university trustee, and as the author of Christian position papers related to medical ethics and biblical creation. He lives with his wife, Shari, and their son and daughter in San Diego, California.

Made in the USA
Monee, IL
15 November 2023